You Are
What You Remember

You Are
What You Remember

*A Pathbreaking Guide to Understanding
and Interpreting Your Childhood Memories*

PATRICK ESTRADE

TRANSLATED BY LEAH BRUMER

Da Capo
LIFE
LONG

A Member of the Perseus Books Group

Copyright © 2006 Éditions Robert Laffont
Translation © 2008 Perseus Books Group, Inc.

Designed by Pauline Brown
Set in 11 point Berkeley Book by the Perseus Books Group

Library of Congress Cataloging-in-Publication Data

Estrade, Patrick.
  You are what you remember : a pathbreaking guide to understanding and interpreting your childhood memories / Patrick Estrade ; translated by Leah Brumer.
        p.   cm.
  "First published in France in 2006 by Éditions Robert Laffont."
  Includes bibliographical references and index.
  ISBN 978-1-60094-042-2 (alk. paper)
  1. Psychoanalysis. 2. Recollection (Psychology) 3. Children. I. Title.
  RC506.E83513 2008
  616.89'17—dc22

                                                                      2008014605

First Da Capo Press edition 2008
First published in France in 2006 by Éditions Robert Laffont. This edition is published by arrangement with Éditions Robert Laffont.

Ouvrage publié avec le soutien du Centre National du Livre—ministère français chargé de la culture. / Work published with the support of the Centre National du Livre—French Ministry of Culture.

Published by Da Capo Press
A Member of the Perseus Books Group
www.dacapopress.com

Da Capo Press books are available at special discounts for bulk purchases in the United States by corporations, institutions, and other organizations. For more information, please contact the Special Markets Department at the Perseus Books Group, 2300 Chestnut Street, Suite 200, Philadelphia, PA 19103, or call (800) 810-4145, extension 5000, or e-mail special.markets@perseusbooks.com.

1 2 3 4 5 6 7 8 9

To Georgette

Contents

Part Three: How to Read and Interpret Childhood Memories

Part Five: Discovering Your History

Foreword

I N MY LAST BOOK, I analyzed the forms of resistance and the defense mechanisms we create to avoid suffering.[1] I showed how unconscious programming and isolation lead us to mistake resistance for personality. In this book, I address issues of the human spirit and how we live by examining the emotional dimension of memories and how they relate to our present life.

Many thinkers and writers have examined childhood memories over the past decades. Sigmund Freud is, of course, among the most renowned. However, I believe Alfred Adler is the person whose genius and study have made the greatest contribution to this issue. He gave us several important interpretations of memories, in particular, his book, *The Practice and Theory of Individual Psychology,* published in Germany in 1928. To my knowledge, no other work addresses memory as I do here apart from certain aspects of Adler's book.

My book is based on notes of memories told to me over a period of twenty-five years and on the system I developed to organize, analyze and interpret them. The clinical cases presented here are drawn from my professional experience. As always, I have changed the names and other personal details of the individuals quoted to protect their privacy. I asked each person, whether patient or friend, for permission to include him or her in this book. Their responses were identical. "If my story can increase understanding of your work and help others, I am happy to participate." I would like to thank them.

Our memories, both good and bad, are inextricably linked to our deepest selves. They are the guardians of our innermost sanctuary, just as Freud said that our dreams are the guardians of our sleep. Our memories speak to us, but what do they say? They tell of what we were and what we experienced. Perhaps most importantly, they also tell us how we lived those experiences. Our memories speak to us, but we do not listen. That is because, as with dreams, we do not know how.

In this book, I want to show you that our memories are consistent with our present style of life and, as a result, how they influence us and may prevent us from growing and changing. I also want to show you the relationship between the past contained in our memories and our experiences today and, finally, how memories can shed light on our behavior and help us achieve self-knowledge and self-transcendence.

I refer often in this book to the family constellation, including parents, siblings and grandparents. You may be surprised that my comments do not address the specific situation of children who have lost their parents, but I want to avoid the mistake of assuming that family structure determines fate, which can lead to clichéd conclusions. Individual lives can take very different paths. One child who enters the child welfare system might be shunted from facility to facility or end up in a cold or indifferent foster family, while another might live and flourish in a warm and loving adoptive family. Thus we cannot generalize or reduce this issue to legal status. Losing your parents does not mean that you grew up without a family, that you did not experience childhood or that you lack memories of that time. If you were orphaned as a child, some of the situations presented in this book will not correspond to your own past. However, you will be able to adapt my ideas to your situation easily.

A Note to Readers

Will You Join Me?

Before getting to the heart of the matter, I would like to invite you to conduct a small experiment. Have I piqued your curiosity? First, find a piece of paper and a pen. Please concentrate and allow a memory from your early childhood to rise to the surface. Reach back as far as you can. Don't actively search among your memories, don't censor yourself and don't choose one over another. It doesn't matter whether your memory is positive or negative, an actual one or one that your parents or a close relative told you. It's not particularly important if it dates back to your early childhood or a bit later. What is important is that you write it down just as it comes to you. Don't write more than a few words and, above all, don't dress it up with fancy adjectives or well-turned phrases. We want your spontaneous recollection, okay?

Now repeat the exercise and write down another memory. I'm still looking for the oldest one possible. Is the exercise a little easier this time? That's normal, since you've had some practice.

And now, please write down a third, following the same rules. Try to reach back as far as you can. Don't think too hard, censor yourself or use too many words.

Last, since you never know, go ahead and take advantage of the moment and write down a fourth.

I know, this isn't what you expected. You thought you were just going to settle down with a good book. What's more, some of you might not have wanted to follow my directions, either because you're lazy ("Hey, that's rude!"), suspicious ("What's this all about?") or impatient ("I don't want to!"). It doesn't matter. No one is forcing you to do anything. Others may not have managed to write down a single memory that seemed important. Perhaps you found yourself staring into a big black hole. Don't worry, I'll get to that later.

Once you've written your four memories, you may go back to each one and add as many details as you like. However, to distinguish between the core memory and the added details, underline the former, use a different color ink or write it in capital letters. That's what I did with my three memories. I will discuss them with you later.

Why didn't I give you more time to warm up for the experiment? You'd rather that I waited until the end of the book? Well, sorry. You know as well as I do that when we take a test, we like to know where it's going. We don't like to feel insecure, so we try to anticipate the questions and come up with a general outline that we'll flesh out when we actually sit down to write. That's just what I wanted to avoid. I didn't want the information presented later in this book to influence you so that you would try to be more "objective" in thinking about your memories. That would make them less valuable and useful, although when all is said and done, I wonder whether that would really be an issue. But better safe than sorry.

MY THREE EARLIEST MEMORIES

Like you, I wrote the first three memories that came to mind, putting them down immediately, without thinking, categorizing or censoring. My core memories are in italics and the details are in regular type, like the rest of the text.

My first memory: *I am in a garden that looks slightly neglected. I have a brightly colored butterfly net in my hand and I'm trying to catch the butterflies flitting through the tall grass.*

We are in the Vendée region of France, in my Uncle Jean and Aunt Jeanne's garden. There's a henhouse at the far end of the garden. It's a sunny day and I'm wearing shorts. The butterfly net is made of a long wooden handle with a circle of wire attached to it at one end. I don't remember whether the net was red or yellow, but I know it was a bright color. It's a little stiff, as if it had been starched.

The second memory that came to mind was when my sister, Annick, fell down the stairs. She was riding on my brother Yves's back and she broke an upper tooth when she fell.

This occurred in the house where we lived when I was very young. As best as I can remember, the staircase was very narrow. There were no bathrooms upstairs, so you had to go downstairs to use the toilet. That scared me when I had to get up in the night.

I was told that the accident occurred because I was tickling them and they lost their balance. That broken tooth really upset my sister. For years, she refused to smile when she had her picture taken. That's probably when responsibility and guilt became issues for me.

In my third memory, my mother and I were at the market when she suddenly burst into tears.

This was a covered market in Nice, France. No one else was with us. I was very young and it upset me to see her cry. I said, "Don't cry, Mommy."

We'll stop our experiment there for now. You may come back to each of your memories as often as you like and take another look at them, using the tools I will provide in the following chapters. I'll talk more about my memories later on.

Part One

Memory and Memories

CHAPTER 1

Memories Offer
a World of Infinite Riches

What matters in life is not what happens to you, but
what you remember and how you remember it.
—GABRIEL GARCÍA MÁRQUEZ,
LIVING TO TELL THE TALE

M Y PROFESSION HAS many wonderful dimensions. The people I see in my practice share their worlds with me. Each is infinitely rich and beautiful, even if painful events led those individuals to my office. When a trusting relationship exists, it's as if the patient gives me the keys to her house and allows me to come and go freely and wander from room to room. Of course, psychotherapists don't go around peeking into closets out of some unhealthy curiosity. They are there to serve the patient.

This kind of trust is not built instantaneously. That would be inappropriate for the patient, the psychotherapy and the psychotherapist, who would recognize it as signaling a problem in

3

the transference process. While gaining the patient's trust immediately might gratify the psychotherapist, blind trust is never a
good thing. Trust is built on what the therapist gives as a professional and as a human being. As a result, it is highly subjective.
We all have our own ways of creating the conditions in which
trust can develop. Of course, there's the setting of the psychotherapist's office—the building, the waiting room and the
consulting room where patient and therapist meet. Other factors
include the sense of empathy the therapist conveys and the way
he or she approaches the patient and asks questions. Clues to the
psychotherapist's professional world are visible to the visitor
(which psychological or psychoanalytic school of thought does
he or she subscribe to?), and the therapist may reveal information
about his or her private life (including hobbies, interests, tastes
and books). Last, there is the psychotherapist's personal work
that can benefit the patient—the effort devoted to the therapist's
own growth. I once heard a speaker at a psychology conference
in Berlin say, "Patients can learn from a psychotherapist only that
which the therapist has been able to accomplish." That short sentence helped me grasp what lay ahead of me. I took it as an ad-
monition to us as students not to be satisfied with seeing patients
but to continue studying and learning.

MY MISTAKE AS A NEW THERAPIST

Memories are among the most moving aspects of the worlds that
patients share with psychotherapists. I did not recognize that
when I was new to the field. I treated patients' memories as part

of the medical history that helped me make a diagnosis or revealed a neurosis. Although it is painful to admit, during those years I would ask my patient for a childhood memory in the same routine tone of voice that doctors use when they ask a patient to get undressed. Alfred Adler always asked his new patients to tell him their first memory.[1] That should have alerted me to the importance of memories, but I ignored the information. Only gradually, as months passed and I became a better listener, did I begin to perceive the language of memories and discover its essential nature.

Patients must have told me at least two thousand memories during the early years of my practice in Berlin. Learning to interpret them in the context of the individual's entire life helped me the most. When I returned to France in the early 1980s, I refined my method of understanding and interpreting childhood memories and realized that I had developed my own psychological and psychotherapeutic tool.

READING MEMORIES IS AN ART

Reading memories is an art that takes practice. The questions must focus quickly but without rushing or offending the patient. That would create resistance immediately and put the psychotherapist on the wrong track.

Professor Josef Rattner of the Analytical Psychology Institute in Berlin used to say that the task required a Sherlock Holmes crossed with Sigmund Freud and Mephistopheles: Holmes for his exceptional knowledge that allowed him to establish unexpected and remarkable connections, as well as for his humble deductive genius ("Elementary, my dear Watson!"); and Freud for the notion of free-floating attention,[2] the ability to avoid focusing exclusively on the individual's description of symptoms and, instead, experience the fullness of the "being there" and open oneself completely to listening. Mephistopheles reminds us to guard against the tendency to see good and evil as separate and absolute. Each is present in the other, as life illustrates so powerfully.

I would add a fourth to this trio: the phenomenologist. In philosophy, the "phenomenon" is the object or event that is perceived by the senses. The phenomenologist's perception involves setting aside, for the moment, what we know and project so that we can pay attention, fully and straightforwardly, to what we are given to see and hear. The task is thus to understand, not explain.[3]

With this precaution in mind, I learned to see memories differently over the years. The process has been richly rewarding. I gradually developed a methodology that takes a practical approach to memories and immediately allows me to get to the heart of the issue the individual is facing. While my patients were surprised by my ability to read and analyze their situations, my own observations often dumbfounded me, prompting me to use this fascinating—and risky—tool with particular caution and care. I regularly replay Friedrich Nietzsche's warning in my mind: "The supposed 'shorter ways' have always put mankind into great danger; at the glad tidings that such a shorter way has been found, they always desert their way—and *lose their way*."[4] Thus I was not particularly disappointed when, in 1990, a university lecture I was supposed to give on the subject of memory was canceled. I took it to mean that my approach to memories was not yet fully developed. The time wasn't right.

MEMORIES ARE A TREASURE CHEST

When childhood memories are not marked by a terrible event, they are extraordinary emotional nooks and crannies—dazzling, surprisingly funny, intelligent, tender and mischievous. They speak of life in all its simplicity and its complexity. That makes sense. How many lives do we live in one lifetime? Three? Five? Ten? More? If I examine my own life, I can count eleven so far, beginning with the house where I was born and continuing to my family's first move, my elementary school years, my childhood Catholic education, boarding school, my experiences as a young man, my time in Berlin, the years with M. (a woman I was involved with in the early 1970s), my early career in Nice, my life with my wife and son and my life as a writer. Each one contributed, in its own way, to transforming the child, young man and adult that I was and that I am. How many more lives will I have? I don't know and, to be honest, I don't worry about it.

It is difficult to imagine the wealth inherent in the memories that psychotherapists hear over the course of their practice. These memories are always characterized by honesty, depth and emotion. They are like exquisite lace or finely crafted silver because they are told with the heart of a child. When we talk about childhood memories, we are referring to the child living within us, the child we try so hard to hide, the one who takes us by the hand and leads us back in time. "Do you remember?" the child asks. "Enough," the adult says. "I don't give a damn about that. That's in the past." (Adults are convinced they have more important things to do than remember their foolish acts from long ago.) "You don't give a damn?" the child asks. "That's impossible. If you only knew how much baggage you're carrying!" Whether we believe it or not, we do spend time thinking about our childhood. It binds us with a thousand invisible ties—our memories.

They are the indelible stamp of our individuality, our signature and the proof that what we experienced is ours alone and will never belong to anyone else. We are all that we remember and all that we do not remember because the feeling has been imprinted on our emotional memory. (To *imprint* means to record a perception in memory.)

That's what happens to childhood tricks, open secrets, puppy loves, little lies and youthful acts of disobedience. Bursting with laughter, a young woman recently told me how she once tricked her parents, who had forbidden her to let her boyfriend into the house when they were not home. She managed to sneak him in and then out again when her mother came back unexpectedly. She laughed until she cried, remembering how he had to pass through every room until he reached the door as she led her mother to the other side of the house, diverting her attention with a series of ridiculous questions.

Childhood is full of those tricks, crushes, secrets, lies and pseudo-dangers. When I walked down the street with my parents as a child, I made up all sorts of games that I now realize were superstitions and rites. My poor parents had no idea about the horrible fate we avoided at every step. The risk was as deadly as it was obvious. My game followed the rules of hopscotch and I had to avoid stepping on the lines in the sidewalk at all costs. If I crossed the line, everything would be lost. At first glance, this might seem easy. Maybe you think all I needed to do was keep a steady pace. But you're missing the unknowns along the way— a big dog that heads in your direction at a trot, grown-ups who bump into you, or a stroller that bears down on you. You've got to react constantly to all these unknowns, revise your pace with every step, consider the length of the step you just took as you anticipate the next one and prepare to take a giant one that will launch you smack into the middle of the next square, which will set you up for a regular-size step into the following one. Kafka and Shakespeare rolled up in one! If I didn't follow the rules, my family and I risked car accidents, painful illnesses, sudden death. And when my worst fear was finally realized and no disaster followed, I would tell myself that we owed our lives to God's infinite indulgence.

I sometimes think about that even now when I'm walking down the sidewalk. I try to reexperience the wonderful shiver of danger I felt then. When I watch people in the street, sometimes I see a person whose step hesitates just like mine.

Memories are chains that bind us to a particular perception of ourselves, but they also represent a unique and precious place where we can be free, a private space that no one may enter without our consent. This can irritate inquisitive family members and partners who would like to monitor us constantly, down to our very thoughts and memories. "What are you thinking about?" "Oh, nothing," we answer, drifting off as we reminisce. We don't say a word except, perhaps, a little lie or silly excuse that ends the conversation.

OUR MEMORIES ARE THE TENDER SPOT
THAT OUR EXPERIENCES LEAVE BEHIND

Our lives are swathed in memories that form our internal skin. Even so, we cannot begin to imagine what is hidden in the act of remembering. It is a very ordinary action but often flirts with the limits of the unconscious. Daily life does not offer many opportunities to consciously recall memories. A smell, an image, a sound or a chance event may call up the glimmer of a memory, but we must allow it to enter our consciousness, rise to the surface and flood through us. We don't do that, whether for lack of time or simply because the situation does not lend itself to such an exercise. (Personally, I have a hard time giving myself over to memories while shopping for groceries or stuck behind the wheel in traffic.) We make room for our memories only under certain circumstances, when we are relaxed, at ease or otherwise disengaged (for example, in a waiting room or on a bus or train). Sometimes we are not even aware of what we are doing. When we enter that state of semiawareness, the unconscious plays hide-and-seek with the conscious. "That smell of coffee . . . that's what it smelled like at home when I would get back from basketball practice and my mother was waiting for me to go to the store." Existing barely at the level of consciousness, the memory drifts to the surface and brushes lightly against us, like a fish that nibbles bait without grabbing it. The light attached to the memory flickers but does not attract our attention. That's lucky, because if we were systematically aware of our memories, they would harass us, grab us, hold us hostage and prevent us from going about our lives. The unconscious wisely sorts things out for us. French philosopher Henri Bergson described it this way: "The brain serves rather to recall the memory, not conserve it." Further on, he wrote, "Such is the role of the brain in the functioning of memory: it does not conserve the past, but first masks it and then allows what has practical use to be revealed."[5]

The brain recalls a memory based on what we experienced, whether consciously or unconsciously, in terms of what did or did not happen. It follows a rule similar to the unities of classical theater, which require unity of place, time and action. I would add "feeling" to that list. If a memory is to exist, it must call up a feeling, no matter how slight. "To remember is to feel what one has felt," English philosopher Thomas Hobbes wrote.[6] But is that enough? A parlor game that involves telling memories may be fun for an evening, but it hardly qualifies as digging deep into the subject. I remember seeing the actor Samy Frey perform George Perec's work titled, fittingly, *Je me souviens* (I Remember) at the Théâtre de la Madeleine in Paris. Seated on his bicycle, Frey recited, one by one, the 480 memories that make up the text. It begins, "I remember dinners at the big bakery table. Soup with milk in winter, soup with wine in summer. I remember the free gift in the box of Bonux soap powder that my sister and I fought over until the next box of detergent was purchased, I remember the bananas cut in three—there were three of us." The actor did a fine job, but I felt there was something slightly dehumanizing and Kafkaesque about the whole thing. It must have been the sheer volume of the memories recounted and the fact that with rare exceptions, the audience did not have the same experiences, so we could not savor sharing them with Perec. However, when he did touch a common memory, everyone laughed enthusiastically.[7]

Our memories include everything we have ever felt, the positive and the negative. They include the good that finally came from pain, the sad memories of leaving a happy time or place and the nostalgia we continue to feel. You can strip people of everything, violate their privacy, seize what is most important to them and leave them with nothing, but you cannot steal their memories.

Memories belong to our individual unconscious. According to Swiss psychiatrist C. G. Jung, "The personal unconscious contains lost memories, painful ideas that are repressed (that is, forgotten intentionally), subliminal perceptions, by which are meant sense-perceptions that were not strong enough to reach consciousness and, finally, contents that are not yet ripe for consciousness." [8] Images he calls "archetypes" probably play a role in the delicate process of creating memories. "These personal reminiscences are manifestations that emanate from the deepest layers of the unconscious, layers where the original images, humanity's endowment, lie dormant."[9] Others go further. For example, some followers of shamanism believe that each person carries the memories of every human experience throughout evolution, including what we have seen and eaten since the origin of the species. I wouldn't go that far.

THE OBJECTS THAT BUTTRESS OUR MEMORIES

Memories are buttressed by the eponymous objects they refer to, from a porcelain dish to a carved pipe, plastic flowers, souvenir glass, snow globe or T-shirt, not to mention postcards, books, maps, brochures and the paper napkins from the little restaurant across from City Hall that we tucked away like treasured relics. And don't forget the camera we used to immortalize grandma and the kids eating ice cream in front of the Statue of Liberty.

You think I'm exaggerating? Put the book down and look around your own "home sweet home." You'll see that my list is quite conservative. But rest assured—I'm no different. From my desk chair, I can see a black stone scarab with hieroglyphic carvings that came directly from Egypt, a Native American dream catcher that my sister, Annick, brought back from Canada, a pitcher from Venice, a fan purchased at the Maeght Foundation on the French Riviera, not to mention a magnificent Bavarian beer mug crammed with pens, pencils, scissors (I remember buying those at Skansen Park in Stockholm) and a variety of highlighters. The mug is practical but awfully tacky.

I find the offices of doctors, lawyers and other highly trained professionals to be a treasure trove of souvenirs. Even to the minimally trained eye, they reveal a great deal about the person's life. (While no one is immune from the tendency to collect such objects, employees in hierarchical organizations may not have the freedom to display their collections.)

Do you have any idea how many souvenirs the average person amasses in a lifetime? Do you know how many reproductions the little souvenir shop at the base of the Eiffel Tower or the Statue of Liberty sells? What about the profits generated by the souvenir market in a country like France or the United States? It must be in the billions of dollars. Why are they so popular? Because these experiences touch us at an emotional level and we want to immortalize them. It is discouraging to think that the memories of our most remarkable experiences could exist alongside ordinary, trivial and mediocre mass-produced objects. Kitsch reigns in the souvenir market. What is kitsch? The characteristic expression of emotional overinvestment. The quasi-unconscious part of our sentimental world fixates on a trivial object that is nevertheless important because it bears visible witness to our lives, existence and experiences, both good and bad. Eight years after I broke my wrist, I still have the pin the surgeon removed after the break healed. Why would I hold on to that sharp piece of metal? It must play some role, but I don't really know.

We all have relics, fetishes and treasures, not to mention decorative objects, ashes and tombs. They may be visible or invisible, external or internal, sublimely beautiful or ridiculously kitschy. This tangible evidence underscores the importance of our experiences, granting them legitimacy. You can't argue with that.

THE MEMORIES THAT CONCERN US HERE

Our memory objects have nothing to do with aesthetics. Rather, and most importantly, they express what is close to the heart.

When the heart speaks, it does so simply, straightforwardly and unreservedly. The memories I discuss in this book are not the ones we share with our friends. Those are the stories we tell. Some have happy endings and others don't. The memories we will explore here are linked to the mysteries of the soul and the spirit, psyche and heart.

Those are the ones that interest me. I know I will stir up old feelings and recollections you have buried deep inside. They are sensitive and wonderful, moving and startlingly beautiful. They may be sad, harrowing, unhappy and terrifying, too. You may have buried them deep down so that you don't have to think about them. You may have packed them away with those old songs you grew tired of hearing. Perhaps they wounded or bruised you or left you in suspense, as if hanging by a thread. Memories are that and more.

No One Is Neutral About Childhood Memories

As soon as you raise the subject of memories, everyone offers an opinion. One person has lots of memories, another has none, a third thinks they're unimportant, a fourth does not. And so on. Some subjects seem to interest everyone. We won't necessarily agree, but we'll have a lively discussion. If you're at a party and conversation is lagging, turn the talk to childhood memories and you'll see. The people seated around you will perk up immediately. No one is neutral when it comes to childhood memories because they are the daybooks of our lives (those huge ledgers where daily accounting transactions are recorded). But this ledger is unusual: it's not an accurate account of everything we have experienced but an accurate—sometimes too accurate—account of the experiences we think are important. I remember talking to a woman who started crying as she recalled a terrible argument between her parents. In a moment of rage, her father, whom she said she idolized, burst out, "I don't give a damn about my daughter, do you understand? I don't give a damn!" You and I know that any of us could say those words thoughtlessly, without ever expecting that they would plant a seed. However, they had a profound impact on this woman, who took them to mean that her father did not love her. His subsequent acts of caring and tenderness never managed to make up for the verbal wound he inflicted in a moment of frustration. Rebuilding his image, deeply damaged by this unfortunate outburst from a husband probably frustrated by his wife's effort to preserve their marriage, took many therapy sessions.

We keep very careful accounts of our emotional past, but we are not good accountants. We select the memories that matter to us and "forget" those we want to be rid of. Nietzsche, who was a great psychologist as well as a philosopher, reminds us, "'I have done that,' says my memory. 'I cannot have done that,' says my pride and remains unshakeable. Finally, memory yields."[10] Yes, memory yields when yielding does not cause too much pain.

We all have our own way of cataloguing our memories. If there are good reasons to remember something, then it seems important. That's obvious. However, we remember many situations, experiences and events of minimal importance. As with dreams, however, what may be insignificant for the conscious may have great significance for the unconscious.

Part Two

*Tapping the
Well of Memories*

CHAPTER 2

Dreams and Memories

Strange are these creatures, strange indeed,
Who what's unfathomable, fathom,
What never yet was written, read,
Knit and command the tangled mystery
And in the eternal dark yet find a way.
—HUGO VON HOFMANNSTHAL, *DEATH AND THE FOOL*

THE FREUDIAN LEGACY

Many experts have researched the subject of memory. But as far as I know, few have examined memories and their dynamic, living structure, probably because they are linked to the singularly subjective world of emotions, sensations and feelings. We see this as a realm of poetic and literary expression, rather than an area of scientific investigation. Of course, that doesn't stop psychoanalysts from putting memories under their magnifying glass.

Even so, dreams enjoy higher status, since they have always captivated humans. Kings and slaves alike have tried to grasp their meaning and even use them to read the future. Who would turn that down? But the language of dreams is so unsettling and subjective that many have preferred to consult the stars, an approach that has proven surprisingly revealing since ancient times, particularly when seeking to predict the future and change fate. Assuming, of course, that you're a believer! Dreams only emerged from their prescientific epoch in 1926, when Freud published his dazzling work, *The Interpretation of Dreams,* and offered an initial scientific approach worthy of the term.[1] Of course, others had conducted considerable work prior to that time. The chronological bibliography at the end of Freud's work offers some surprises. The twenty-three-page bibliography—including references from Achmetis' *Oneirocritica,* published in 1603, to Moshe Wulff's 1913 work on the relationship between dreams, symbols and symptoms of illness—reveals the breadth of scientific interest in understanding dreams and provides evidence of its scientific rigor, as if that were necessary.[2]

One of Freud's fundamental contributions to the study of dreams was the distinction he drew between what he called their manifest content and their latent content. In simple terms, the dream's manifest content is what can be explained or recounted (for example, a child who is denied dessert and dreams of a gingerbread house). The latent content is what the unconscious has reworked, the job he called the "dream work." Latent content cannot be deciphered without the ability to interpret, which Freud did so well. In Stefan Zweig's book on Freud, the author explains, "We must thus carefully distinguish between two things: that which the dream has 'poeticized' in an effort to veil, what we call the 'dream-work,' and that which conceals true psychological elements behind those opaque veils (that is, the 'dream content')."[3]

The Viennese psychoanalyst addressed the issue of memory many times, focusing on what he called screen memories, among other topics. Referring to work published previously in 1899, he noted that "a person's earliest childhood memories seem frequently to have preserved what is indifferent and unimportant," screening off more essential ones. "They are substitutes, in [mnemic] reproduction, for other impressions that are really significant . . . The memory of these significant impressions can be developed out of the indifferent ones by means of psychical analysis, but a resistance prevents them from being directly reproduced." He compared screen memories to forgetting names. "In the case of forgetting of names we are aware that the substitutive names are incorrect, in concealing memories we are surprised that we have them at all."[4]

ALFRED ADLER'S PERSPECTIVE

Dreams had a different meaning for Alfred Adler. While Freud understood them as the fulfillment of repressed desires, Adler saw them as an opportunity to find solutions to our problems. "People have regarded dreams as offering solutions to their problems. We may conclude that the individual's purpose in dreaming is to seek guidance for the future and to seek a solution to his problems," he wrote.[5] For Adler, the dream's raison d'être is what it evokes emotionally: "The aim of the dream is the feelings it leaves behind."[6] But above all, he sees dreams as "an attempt to make a bridge between an individual's life style and his present problems . . . The life style will always arouse the feelings that the individual needs."[7] I do not propose to choose between these two psychoanalytic pioneers, although my perspective is more Adlerian than Freudian.

Adler devotes a long chapter to early childhood memories in *What Life Could Mean to You.* It deserves close examination, particularly because it inspired the paths my research followed. I have chosen ten of those to discuss with you.

A Link Exists Between Our Earliest Memories and Our Style of Life

In Adlerian psychology, "style of life" refers to how courageously or cautiously we face life events, compensate for feelings of inferiority and assert and position ourselves; how and to what extent we cooperate or compete with others; and how we find our place in the world as we face love, work and other people. Adler calls these the "tasks of life."

The unity of the personality explains why early memories correspond to style of life. Although the individual is multifaceted, personality operates in unified fashion. Just as patients bring their experiences from the outside world into the psychotherapist's office and try to relive their feelings with the therapist (from anger to sulkiness, aggressivity, indifference, seduction, blackmail or expectation of reward), so they bring, along with their oldest memories, the shadings and nuances of their style of life.

Memories Serve the
Same Purpose As Dreams

Memories are a product of our psychic apparatus, the essence of the thoughts, feelings and sensations stored within us. They may be related to buried desires, as Freud noted, or to fears, expectations and hopes. I believe that memories, like dreams, have manifest content and latent content.

- A memory's manifest content arises from the relationship between reality and our conscious (one thing makes me think of another via a chain of connections or via linked thoughts). A memory always includes manifest content because it is triggered by a present event, whether random or recalled and whether perceived strongly or slightly.

- A memory's latent content emerges from the search our unconscious initiates for a memory corresponding to an actual internal emotional state or perception, rather than to a predictable framework. Consequently it is nearly impossible to discern latent content without experience. Until now, only seasoned analysts and therapists have been able to detect, translate and interpret latent content, although interpretation was often difficult and vague because proper tools were not available. Now that those tools are available, interpretation has become much easier.

A Link Exists Between Our Memories and Our Present Situation

Adler had the wisdom to understand this before anyone else. However, as is often the case, the clearest statements can be the hardest to understand. Most therapists thus overlooked the powerful signposts that memories represent because they failed to grasp their analytic and psychoanalytic significance.

We do not search out a particular memory because we are thinking about the past, but because we are thinking about the present. By examining the kind of memory we do look for, we can gain a greater understanding of our present life. In their book about memory, Jean-Yves and Marc Tadié write, "We never remember a memory in the same way that we remember how to type. Rather, we recreate the memory based on the context at the moment it was stored in memory and on our current context."[8] They recognized the dimension of re-creation that emerges in the encounter between an external circumstance (something happens to me) and an emotion (that event produces a particular feeling in me). The entire human dialectic is present in that process: the external world and the internal world, conditioning and responsiveness, what is programmed and what is created. We will come back to this later.

When we analyze the link between memory and experience, we must distinguish between memories expressed spontaneously and freely (for example, when reminiscing with friends about good times spent together) and memories expressed in response to a request (for example, your son asks you to tell him a story from your life). The former originate in a process that focuses primarily on manifest content, while the latter reveals not only the individual's state of mind and situation but how he experienced that situation. I will also return to this point in detail in Chapter 5.

Memories Change Based on the Individual's Style of Life

A woman once came to see me because she felt depressed. She was enmeshed in an endless series of dependency issues and found it difficult to say no. She felt physically ill and experienced nearly constant pain in her limbs. After an effective course of psychotherapy, she said, beaming, "I don't see life in the same way anymore and I don't perceive or feel things in the same way. I've gotten rid of my excess baggage and everything feels lighter. I'm so happy. Everything is clear now. Before, I was like a sponge and absorbed every problem. Now, I can speak my mind and I don't try to take on other people's responsibilities. The oddest thing is that even the past has changed." Of course, her past had not changed but her perception of it had. Because her style of life had evolved, she could seek out other memories and emotions from her past that corresponded with the positive aspects of her present life.

You've heard it said, "Tell me who your friends are and I'll tell you who you are." Our friends and our identity evolve over time, and as we gain self-knowledge our memories change, too. This is particularly striking among people who say they have few memories from infancy and childhood. Psychotherapists know this. These patients have been living in a state we could almost describe as the psychological equivalent of oxygen deprivation, and they experience an extremely low level of emotional consciousness. The therapist's job is to manage the slow process by which they regain full consciousness. This emotional decompression can be painful, emotional and tense, but imagine what it feels like when one, two, three and even more memories rush back, like letters that have been waiting at the post office while you've been away.

The Age and Nature of an Individual's Earliest Memory Reveal His Fundamental Attitude Toward Life

The age and nature of a person's earliest memory reveal the extent to which he has been able to grasp and master the whole of his life. However, the age of the memory is not always essential. If you don't have vivid memories from before the age of eight or ten, you're not excluded. Memories are like fish. Some flit across the surface of the water and can be seen easily, while others remain in the depths. They may not be immediately visible, but they are still there.

Childhood Memories Provide Reliable Information About the Child's Relationship with His Mother, Father and Other Family Members

I consider this to be a critical, even decisive aspect of the interpretation of memories with respect to how I understand their dynamic, living structure. Early childhood memories reveal elements of the individual's style of life that help us understand a range of personality issues, from constructive to problematic or neurotic. (As Freud observed, "The source of neuroses is to be found in childhood traumas.")[9] If we want to recall early childhood memories, the mind first—and logically—thinks of those related to the home or most intimate setting. In order of importance, they include baby, mother, father, brothers and sisters. However, if your childhood was not peaceful and calm, you might well look somewhere less logical. To the extent that childhood memories provide information about our relationships with close family members, they do so in every sense of the word—including what was present, partially absent (for example, through symbolization in the memory) or absent altogether. The whole art of interpreting memories lies in identifying and giving meaning to that presence, partial absence or total absence.

Many People Ignore Memories That They Consider "Mere Facts" and Are Unaware of Their Hidden Meaning

Like dreams, slips of the tongue and subconsciously deliberate mistakes, memories are anything but mere facts. While they may not speak to the average person, that's because he does not know how to listen to and decipher them. Adler explained it clearly. "Scarcely anyone understands a first memory, and most people are therefore able to confess their purpose in life, their relationships with others and their view of the environment in a perfectly neutral and natural manner through their first memories."[10] That is still true today.

To Understand Memories, We
Must Learn the "Art of Divining"

To divine is to discover by intuition or insight or to perceive intuitively. Perhaps this term helps explain why Adler has not always received the attention he deserves. As he was the first to show, interpreting memories is hardly a guessing game. It may be an art, but it is based on a method. That art involves understanding what a detail reveals when examined in the context of the whole and, conversely, what the whole can reveal about a particular detail. Philosophy refers to this as the hermeneutic circle. I believe that interpreting memories involves both art and methodological process.[11]

Memories Allow Us to
Stabilize Our Emotional States

Our emotional states adjust to memories. We seek out a memory reflecting a mood or environment that matches the current one, so a melancholy period will correspond to melancholy memories and a shift in the environment at work will correspond to memories of other workplaces. This stabilizing effect is interesting because it demonstrates that our psychological apparatus possesses the resources necessary to restore its equilibrium, showing that the brain is more than a supercomputer. It is also an intelligent, self-regulating machine when it comes to dealing with itself.

Life Is an Extension of
Experiences Within the Family

According to Adler, the child develops a particular style of life between the age of three and four based on a range of parameters, including the mother's and father's presence or absence, birth order or place in the family constellation, health problems, courage or caution in dealing with life and development of a feeling of community or a sense of inferiority. I sometimes refer to this, jokingly, as our personal goodwill. If nothing challenges the individual's style of life, the child-turned-adult may continue to live accordingly for years or even a lifetime. Some people believe this means that the early years determine an individual's life, but I don't think we need to go that far.[12] It is important to remember that psychological issues are never resolved once and for all, or at any particular moment. New attitudes and resolutions can always correct or compensate for mistakes along the way.

Childhood is the prototype for adult life, composed of a collection of experiences and encounters and shaped by disappointments, failures and successes. Over time, this prototype is transformed, changed, added to, improved and adjusted. Little by little, those modifications come to form a specific personality, similar to others in many ways but still unique. The individual's family, community and, simultaneously, personal experiences are planted in the soil that is our inheritance and will be grafted onto a unique rootstock that will finally constitute the adult person. If this process occurs under positive conditions, the individual will find his place in the human community and understand the need for cooperation, while preserving his self-esteem. However, if obstacles block the way, that place will be hard to find and he will develop a personality deficiency that he will seek to compensate for in some way. As defined by the National Association for Self-Esteem, self-esteem is based on security, identity, a sense of belonging, determination and competence.[13] The child first needs security, both external and internal, which provides a strong foundation for constructing an identity that allows him to know and acknowledge himself ("I am unique and different"). The child can then turn to others with a positive attitude and sense of belonging ("I am important to others"), learn to set and pursue goals and take on projects that give his life hope and meaning, thus creating a sense of competence. Developmentally appropriate challenges allow the child to recognize his abilities and value as an individual. Our memories are a product of, and are linked to, our childhood experiences as individuals and within the family and community.

As adults, we are expected to be able to respond to life in its entirety, present, future and past. How we interpret our life allows us to incorporate and integrate our experiences.

To answer the question I pose in this volume—How do memories govern our lives?—I had to define and limit the issues I would address. Because my approach to memories includes innovative aspects, my methodology had to be extremely rigorous and I felt it was critical to clarify the contributions of my renowned predecessors. To interpret means to explain or present in understandable terms and to convey meaning from one language to another, but it remains an eminently subjective act. The Italians have a saying, "Traduttore, traditore," or, "Translator, traitor." Any interpretation can be a betrayal. As a result, strange books may end up occupying the same shelf as serious scientific works. When interpretation ventures into the realm of memory (or any other), it must maintain an analytic approach and not drift into prophecy or revelation.

CHAPTER 3

Memory, Memories and Forgetting

Forgetting and remembering are not symmetrical.
—PAUL RICOEUR, INTERVIEW BY JEAN BLAIN

WHEN IT COMES to memory, we are not all created equal. Some people have a prodigious memory, while others have problems organizing their ideas and memories coherently. Freud placed himself in the former group. "When I was a schoolboy I took it as a matter of course that I could repeat by heart the page I had been reading; and shortly before I entered the university I could write down practically verbatim the popular lectures on scientific subjects directly after hearing them."[1] Few people possess such remarkable abilities.

WHY DO SO FEW PEOPLE HAVE MEMORIES FROM THE FIRST TWO OR THREE YEARS OF LIFE?

An article on the newborn infant's memories (note the plural) in the April–July 2001 issue of *Pour la science*, the French edition of

Scientific American, noted a paradox. Why do children display what Freud called infantile amnesia, which in adulthood prevents them from remembering experiences from the first three or four years of life? After all, infants have a remarkable memory system and early experiences only strengthen it. Researchers who study long-term memory in infants have concluded that while the brain structures required to store memories do exist and are partially functional in the newborn, the infant's memory system is still immature. In addition, events that occur during infancy lack the retrieval cues associated with objects that would allow the infant to anchor the recollection more concretely in her memory. Infantile amnesia is thus a function of lack of access to the memory and an immature memory system.

However, not all research leads to the same conclusion. Researchers have performed interesting experiments with infants on learning and recall, using rattles, mobiles and wind chimes to test their memory. In an article on infants' memories, Carolyn Rovee-Collier and Scott A. Adler described a study of auditory location. "The results show that certain experiences dating back to the infant's prelingual period are retained for a period of up to two years." Further on, they note, "The memory ability of newborns and infants is much more developed than previously recognized and is not fundamentally different from that of older children or normal adults." In their conclusions on infantile amnesia, the two postulate that "the inability of adults to remember experiences from infancy cannot be attributed to memory insufficiency among newborns and very young children. . . . Infants' memories may be preserved long after they acquire language, which excludes the infantile amnesia hypothesis."[2] So much for Freud's notion.

Our earliest memories follow no rules. While most of us have no memories from before the age of four or five, others retain specific and "indisputable" memories from the age of one and a half to two years, which often annoys parents unwilling to believe the child's memories could reach so far back. They avoid the issue by claiming that the youngster must have heard someone talking about the event and remembers the conversation, not the event itself. This can be a painful experience; since it implies that the individual is lying, and it may even be experienced as a denial of the person himself.

We are all different. No one's memory resembles anyone else's. Some people have a prodigious memory, just as some have memories that date back very early in life. The explanation for those differences remains a mystery.

WHY DOES MEMORY WEAKEN WITH AGE?

Until recently, researchers were not particularly interested in human memory. In his introduction to a special issue on memory published by *La recherche,* a French science magazine, Professor Edouard Zarifian wrote, "Twenty years ago, there was no research funding for Alzheimer's disease in France. Fifteen years ago, families didn't even dare talk about it. The first drug, tacrine, came on the market nine years ago. Today, family advocacy groups are making themselves heard, patients are speaking out, economic costs have been calculated and long-term care issues have become a political priority. The era of silence, shame, resignation and inevitability is over."[3] As is often the case, new medical knowledge emerges from a focus on a particular disease, and Alzheimer's is one. Research on the brain and memory has increased dramatically, with a prestigious scientific publication announcing a new advance almost weekly. Progress is now measured month to month—if not week to week—rather than year to year. Similarly, neuroscience and medical imaging offer new understanding of brain mechanisms and diseases. In November 1993, a U.S.-Swedish research team showed that under certain conditions, areas of the brain can regenerate, challenging conventional wisdom that we are born with a fixed number of brain cells that can never be replaced.[4] That finding could be extremely useful in the fight against degenerative neurological diseases like Alzheimer's, Parkinson's, multiple sclerosis and childhood dystonia.

The issue of progressive memory loss concerns all adults as they age and becomes crucial as life expectancy increases. Fearing the onset of Alzheimer's, many people seek medical advice. What does science say?

Opinion is divided. In general, researchers agree that neuronal capacity declines with age. Jean-Yves and Marc Tadié explain that as the frontal lobes atrophy (which can be seen on an MRI), locating the source of information and memories becomes increasingly difficult.[5] However, we know that the number of neurons in the human brain is not fixed and can regenerate. Neuron loss is a bit like hair loss—relative and different from one person to the next. Thus, when Freud wrote that "the command over my memories has steadily deteriorated," we must put his comment in perspective.[6] In fact, he retained a remarkable memory until the end of his life.

Memory is highly individual but is affected by personal commitment and exercise. Attitudes toward life and self-discipline play an important role. And there's the rub. As we age and retirement approaches, the activities that keep us alert and focused are interrupted or come to an end. Daily life becomes increasingly repetitive, reducing the need to call on memory. The problem is even more acute as life expectancy continues to increase. We used to talk about the "young old," then the "old old" and now the "very old old."[7]

The field of psychology has finally recognized the importance of keeping the memory active and vital as we age. Some practitioners organize memory groups where people perform exercises to keep the memory sharp and disciplined.[8]

LONG-AGO MEMORIES VERSUS REMEMBERING WHAT YOU HAD FOR LUNCH YESTERDAY

It's said that with age, memory disappears but memories remain. Why do memories remain? I was one of the first people in France to conduct what I called "geriatric therapy" in a nursing home. I provided group psychotherapy for the elderly, adapted slightly from regular adult group therapy. We would discuss a particular problem in theoretical terms and then I would encourage participants to talk about their concerns. Can you imagine what it was like to manage a group of fifteen people, men and women, ranging in age from seventy-eight to ninety-eight years of age, and from extremely different, if not opposite, backgrounds? Those were extraordinary, formative years for me. You cannot deceive an elderly person—morally, psychologically or philosophically. You must be completely honest because, unless they are ill, they cannot be misled. The best reward I ever received was one day after a group session, when the members came to tell me, "We learned a lot today, Mr. Estrade." I realize that this retirement home was a pioneer in allowing me to hold these sessions. However, we still have a long way to go if we are to incorporate geriatric group therapy into weekly activities at all such facilities.

In my work with elderly people, I was struck by the gap between long-term and short-term memory. Many could recite endless facts about history, geography, literature and math but often found it difficult to tell me what they had just eaten or done that morning. Geriatricians are familiar with this problem and have tried to address it by using memory-enhancing drugs. Research laboratories are studying a variety of approaches, and the fourth-generation drugs appear to be promising. In a February 1999 article on drugs and human memory, Hervé Allain, a neuropharmacist at the University of Rennes, wrote, "Because many changes in the central nervous system related to physiological age and dementia are associated with neuron loss, the use of growth factors to prevent or slow cell death may have a significant impact on preserving memory and other cognitive functions. The current challenge for neuropharmacology is to develop drugs that act on memory processes." That challenge extends beyond drug compounds and includes food supplements. A major market has developed in recent years for various "miracle products" that are supposed to strengthen failing memory. The memory market in the United States is estimated at around $6 billion, with sales of ginkgo biloba at $350 million alone. (The leaves and flowers of the ginkgo biloba have been used in Chinese medicine for four thousand years. Although its mode of action remains unknown, it is thought to work on the circulatory system. By dilating arteries and capillaries, it is claimed to limit the damage caused by oxidation of tissue and brain cells.)

From brain gum (a chewing gum sold on the Internet that is supposed to release an optimizer called phosphatidylserine that prevents memory loss and mental dysfunction) to the now famous omega-3s, new brain-saving products make headline news regularly.[9] In his book *The Instinct to Heal,* David Servan-Schreiber cites the case of a young man, Keith, whose doctors were unable to treat his depression. As a last resort, he was offered a treatment based on purified fish oil. "Nine months later, tests revealed that the metabolism of the young man's brain had been modified," Servan-Schreiber writes. "The membranes of Keith's neurons appeared strengthened and they no longer showed any evidence of leaking valuable constituents . . . The very structure of the patient's brain had been changed."[10]

As noted above, a gap exists between long-term and short-term memory among the elderly. The issue is different for middle-aged people, especially if they are asked to recall something point-blank. Freud raised the issue in the first chapters of *Psychopathology of Everyday Life,* and I have had painful personal experiences with it.[11]

Fifteen years ago, my wife and I attended the summer festival in Avignon, France. We arrived on July 13, the day before the French national holiday, Bastille Day. As we walked down the main street leading to the festival office, a television team stopped us and asked me to sing the first stanza of the French national anthem, "La Marseillaise." Can you guess what happened? "Sure," I said. Isn't that what you'd say if a television reporter stopped you on the street and asked you to sing "The Star-Spangled Banner"? No problem. They moved everyone out of the way, adjusted the sound and the camera and I launched into the song, which I knew by heart. "Allons enfants de la patrie, le jour de gloire est arrivé. . ." Suddenly I drew a blank. "Liberté, liberté chérie . . ." No, that's not how it goes. What comes next? "Contre nous de la tyrannie, l'étendard . . ." Oh yes, of course. But it was too late. My memory had flinched in the face of my emotion. That's obviously what the television team was looking for. Everyone laughed heartily and moved on. But I had to force myself to smile when, two days later, I heard that I had appeared on national news and hundreds of thousands of people had seen me stumble through "La Marseillaise." That's what memory is like. If we appeal to it spontaneously, it serves us well. But if we're under pressure, it lets us down.

THE MEMORY IS LIKE A HUGE WAX RECORDING DISK

Researchers have long been interested not only in how memories are inscribed in the brain, but how and why we retain one memory and not another. Some, like French philosopher Henri Bergson, believe that we remember everything and that all memories stored in our consciousness remain there indefinitely. Others take a different approach. During an annual meeting of the American Association for the Advancement of Science in Boston, Massachusetts Institute of Technology researcher Earl Miller, who studies the frontal cortex and comparative thought, noted that total brain capacity is probably insufficient to preserve every moment of our life in memory.[12] As a result, through evolutionary change, the brain has had to learn to "extract" the points that are common to various experiences and organize them into categories, weighted by usefulness and vital importance. Miller suggests that the brain applies rules that allow us to face new situations, like an animal that must learn to distinguish, recognize and classify the creatures and objects in its environment. This feature reduces the memory work the brain must perform, freeing it from the need to retain all past experiences and preserving only those critical to survival.

That hypothesis seems rational and acceptable, but no scientific proof exists. Why couldn't the brain behave like a computer and zip (compress in order to archive) a record of the information we perceive to store it more efficiently? My view is closer to Bergson's than Miller's. I see the cerebral system as a huge wax disk on which our emotions are engraved. The needle of our existential stylus applies varying degrees of pressure to carve grooves of varying depth into the disk, based on the significance or gravity of the event. If minor, the groove is nearly imperceptible. However, if the experience was intense, the groove is deeper and more precise. A profound existential experience leaves an even deeper furrow, and a traumatic event is marked by a ragged or torn one. The memory of the umbrella pine trees I saw silhouetted against the blue sky on my first visit to the island of Corsica left a mark (as proof, I am telling you about it), but I would describe it as an aesthetic one. On the other hand, the unfair punch I received in the nose when I was seven left a very sensitive—and unaesthetic—mark. (Getting punched in the nose sets off a tear-generating process, which causes you to cry even if the pain is manageable, which increases the feeling of humiliation resulting from the unfair blow and, as a result, increases the flow of tears.) However, neither Corsica's umbrella pines nor the punch in the nose come close to matching the depth of the groove left by my first real kiss, which I experienced walking along the French Riviera one evening with a girl named Corinne.

We perceive particular events as trivial or important based on our personal emotional perception and our personality, which we create throughout life and over the course of our encounters. Those include events we have experienced or caused or have been subjected to, as well as our successes and failures.

My comparison with the wax disk concludes here because our memories are not ledgers, catalogs, photograph albums or stamp collections, nor are they inert. Rather, they swim in the molten material of the universe of our emotions. Like a dormant volcano, they remain potentially active throughout our life. Every emotional situation we experience is positioned and readjusted in relation to all the possible feelings and memories it may trigger. Thus, at this very moment, I am remembering a dam break that occurred in 1959, when I was eleven. I wasn't directly affected, but it was the largest disaster of its kind in France. Why did this thought come to me? Is it the result of an association (volcano→fire→danger→water→danger→dam→break)? That's possible. This example illustrates that the memories within me remain alive, even at the very moment I am speaking to you.

EVERYTHING CAN BECOME A MEMORY

Everything that occurs within the boundaries of our existence or our reach may be a memory and may be recorded as one, beginning with everything that relates to the senses (smell, taste, sight, touch and hearing). I have never reexperienced the taste of the first chocolate bar I bought in Switzerland when I went to summer camp in the mountains. I am sure it was excellent chocolate but in some way, this "nourishing" memory must have also compensated for my mother's absence. Memory also involves everything associated with feelings and emotions. I remember how thrilled I was to give my mother a Mother's Day present (a mirror inside a red felt case). And last, memory involves everything related to both of those. I can remember the sweet fragrance of roses but I also—and more specifically—remember the fragrance of the roses in the garden of my childhood. The blossoms were bigger than my cheeks and I loved to plunge my face into the petals.

We assume that the more powerful the event, the likelier it is to appear on the honor roll of our memories. But our memories are not limited to landmark events. They may also focus on things that appear quite neutral at first (I remember the cupboard door in the entryway) or static (our mailbox was always broken). However, although memories may appear to be insignificant, they have a reason to exist. They evoke something. While they may seem uninteresting initially, they often turn out to be very rich when we relate them to other aspects of life.

We never really know what this "mute" memory is telling us. We may be tempted to think it is irrelevant, but it could be extremely pertinent. We just don't know how to listen to it. Perhaps we have misunderstood or misinterpreted, like witnesses to a crime who give the police varying descriptions of a suspect who has fled.

Everything our wax disk picks up can become a memory, whether the stylus skims lightly, scratches or cuts through. The only requirement is that the event—or, simply put, the thing— be revived and renewed through an encounter with another event or thing, regardless of any direct relationship with the memory. (That would involve what I referred to earlier as the memory's latent content.)

All our memories, whether recalled or forgotten, converge toward the same, single focus: the individual self that experienced the event and the self that remembers it. Everything brings us back to the unity of that self.

However, our unconscious will not always let sleeping memories lie. It can play the spoilsport by leading us to repress or even invent them from whole cloth.

BURIED, REPRESSED AND INVENTED MEMORIES

Like memory, our recollections depend heavily on our interest in them. If, for whatever reason, we ignore or repress them outright, our conscious life cannot express itself with the complexity and richness we have a right to expect. The French have a saying, "Culture is what remains when everything has been forgotten." Similarly, I like to say that emotional equilibrium is what remains when everything has been remembered. We are loath to search out a dark past and sort through painful and difficult moments. As I noted in one of my previous books, the process was not easy for me either.[13]

Everything can be a memory, but every memory can be forgotten. However, "forgotten" does not mean erased or permanently lost, but mislaid somewhere in the maze of memory. A memory may be mislaid randomly when we do not need a particular kind of recollection (for example, the color of Henry IV's horse is irrelevant to me). The unconscious can also cause us to mislay a memory, in which case we would refer to it as repressed. Freud called these screen memories, fragments of memories masking another, buried deeper, that contains repressed content.

People I meet in therapy sessions or at seminars often tell me that they remember almost nothing from before the age of eight, ten or even twelve, as if a heavy curtain covered part of their childhood and could not be lifted. This can be painful, as the individual may feel that part of her childhood, and thus part of her life, has been stolen. However, as Freud said, forgotten memories are not lost. Events that may lead an individual to misplace her memories often occur during difficult, stressful or dangerous periods, whether psychologically, emotionally or physically, which is why the memories cannot find their place in the present. The individual senses that if she were to open the floodgates, all these nightmare memories would rise to the surface and, like a tidal wave, devastate her field of consciousness.

Freud did not consider infantile amnesia to be natural. "We ought to be positively astonished that the memory of later years has as a rule preserved so little of these mental processes, especially as we have every reason to suppose that these same forgotten childhood achievements have . . . exercised a determining influence for the whole of the subject's later life."[14] He agrees with Adler on this point. "Strong forces from later life have been at work on the capacity of childhood experiences for being remembered—probably the same forces which are responsible for our having become so far removed in general from understanding our years of childhood . . . In the so-called earliest childhood memories we possess not the genuine memory-trace but a later revision of it, a revision which may have been subjected to the influences of a variety of later psychical forces."[15]

By referring to "so-called earliest childhood recollections," Freud challenges their authenticity. This is an interesting question. Are memories real, or do we invent them? They are unquestionably filtered through our perceptions, so we must acknowledge their subjectivity. Thus, they may be true as far as we are concerned but not necessarily so with respect to external reality. For proof, just ask a brother or sister to recount a childhood memory. You will notice that the stories are often completely different, if not diametrically opposed. A sibling may even challenge whether a particular episode ever occurred. ("No way, what are you talking about? We never lived with Uncle Ed!")

The accuracy of memories often troubles individuals who are in psychotherapy, particularly when the memories involve another person's guilt. Patients hesitate to challenge someone who is not there to defend himself or herself. In such cases, I explain that psychotherapists know that they never hear "the" truth, but a certain perception of it. The "truth" of the patient's account is less important than the perception of the situation or circumstance that she remembers. Freud called this "the later elaboration of true memory traces." It is important to keep this in mind as you continue reading.

Lost Memories Can Be Found Too

When memories flood back, the experience can be powerful and painful. A young man wrote the following on an Internet discussion site. "I have very painful memories of my childhood that I can't talk about, things that really marked me for life. And that's not all. But what should I do? I feel like I'm stuck."

Sometimes, buried memories must be recalled so that they can be put away for good. That is one of psychotherapy's goals. A new psychotherapeutic technique known as the virtual method was introduced at the seventh Virtual Reality International Conference, held in Laval, France, in April 2005. Psychologist Brenda Wiederhold, director of the Virtual Reality Medical Center in San Diego, California, explained that it involves gradually immersing the patient in a virtual environment corresponding to the stress-generating situation until the patient is able to master her fear, memories or emotions. The patient wears a special helmet and gloves connected to a computer and watches traumatizing scenes in complete security, without leaving the psychologist's office. The psychologist monitors the patient's reactions and guides her through the process. University of Southern California professor Skip Rizzo, who works on cognitive impairment—specifically, problems facing Vietnam and Iraq war veterans—notes, "The results we have obtained are very encouraging, but we should remember that this technique is only a tool. It will never replace a skilled doctor or psychologist."[16]

While traumatic memories that surface may be painful and even shocking, their resilience can represent a remarkable relief. In his book about children and resilience, child psychiatrist Dr. Antoine Guédeney writes, "Resilience is related to the ability to give meaning to a senseless experience and turn it into a coherent narrative. We create narratives for another person, to be understood and accepted (even at the cost of not always being understood perfectly) and to create a connection."[17]

Recovered memories of trauma (particularly cases of incest and sexual abuse, but also attacks like robbery or physical violence) must be entered into the "ledger" so that they can be stored away for good, as memories. As Theresa, one of the first people I treated nearly thirty years ago, wrote to me, "I came to understand that I must give up the pain, separate myself from it and turn it over to the other person—the psychologist sitting across from me—and finally leave it with him, in his office, once and for all."

Recovered memories can also refer to happy events. Through the course of our lives, we encounter a host of memories that emerge during moments of introspection, whether through psychotherapy or just because life prompts us to look within (I'm thinking specifically about what becoming a parent can awaken). A burst of laughter or a scene from childhood or from the elementary school playground may bring a personal memory back to the surface. You might feel a touch of nostalgia and need to take a deep breath to absorb the emotion suddenly sweeping over you. Perhaps the damp fragrance of freshly ironed clothing reminds you of your happiness, as a child, when your mother handed you the steaming iron so that you could iron a handkerchief. That too is life in all its simplicity and beauty. Childhood memories can prompt very serious, scientific consideration but can also move us to poetry and even sentimentality. It's a short hop from Freud to Marcel Proust to *Gone with the Wind*.

As French philosopher Paul Ricoeur explains, "I came to an understanding of forgetting that has two poles. First, there is profound forgetting. That is the erasure of forgetting, the erasure of all traces in the brain. Everything that is a trace may be destroyed. But we may also have the opposite experience: the return of certain memories shows us that we forget less than we believe. You may suddenly remember entire chapters of childhood. I see the field of forgetfulness as a sort of competition between an erasure of forgetting and what I call 'a forgetting kept in reserve.'"[18]

In the end, what is the purpose of forgetting a memory? The answer could not be simpler: to forget. In other words, if I forget, that's because I have good reason to do so. What is the purpose of remembering a memory? To remember. Exactly. Of course, I could say that what we forget are the keys, but in this case, they don't necessarily open the doors we would expect. You might think I'm joking, but I'm serious. Like memories, our forgetting operates within a dialectic. Examining that dialectic, I realized that not only is it "alive" but that a living, dynamic structure underpins it.[19] As far as I know, this structure has never been analyzed systematically in the way I am going to try to analyze it with you.

CHAPTER 4

The Spirit of Our Memories

Childhood is the ground on which we
will walk for our whole life.
—LYA LUFT, *LOSSES AND GAINS*

OUR BURIED MEMORIES HAVE A CHILD'S SPIRIT

Strangely, our memories are stored in our head but preserved in our heart. With a few exceptions, the heart orchestrates and guides our memories, instructing them when to play softly and, if necessary or in case of emergency, when to be silent. Strangely too, it is a child's heart, not an adult's. With its first beat or, if you prefer, first stirrings, probably during its life in utero, that heart created and launched the protocol governing each person's emotional system, translating our earliest perceptions and sensations into emotions and feelings.

Our memories have nothing to do with our chronological age. As Jung wrote, "There is a child in the adult, an eternal child always in a state of becoming, never complete, who needs constant care, attention and education."[1] The emotions linked to our memories come from this child, who is always in a state of becoming. Paradoxically, those emotions are addressed, simultaneously, to that child.

Let's try an experiment. Close your eyes and try to recall a memory. I will too. Here's what I see in my mind's eye. I am on the right-hand path in the garden of the house where I grew up. (There must have been a left-hand path too, but oddly, I don't remember that one.) It's a dirt path and there is a flowering tree. This is the path that leads to the gate. Why did I seek out that memory? Actually, I cheated a bit because I specifically sought a childhood memory. Let me start over. This time, I see a young woman who meant a lot to me. She had a surprised and very gentle expression.

As you can see, my two memories emerge directly from the world of my emotions. I assume the same is true for you. As Antoine de Saint-Exupéry told us, "It is only with the heart that one can see rightly."[2]

THE MOTHER-CHILD DYAD

The mother is the prototype for the child's first relationship.[3] She is the first great "Other" as French psychoanalyst Jacques Lacan would have said. For the mother, the relationship begins before conception, whether she always wanted a child or dreaded the possibility (for fear of pain during childbirth, awkwardness around children in general or simply a decision not to have any). Pregnancy's initial discomforts follow (nausea, tender breasts and fatigue) but as the baby kicks, turns and shifts behind the protective membrane of the mother's belly, those first signs of life quickly make up for them. Until then, the baby can only be imagined, but once it begins to move, it can be represented concretely. Thanks to sonography, the baby can now be seen and even photographed.

From the fourth or fifth month until just before birth, the mother and child will communicate in his or her own way. This contact is a reality, not just a tender notion. Dutch researcher Frans Veldman is considered the father of haptonomy, which he defines as "the science of affectivity," the science of human emotional relations and interactions. Catherine Dolto-Tolitch is one of the most active advocates of perinatal haptonomy. Veldman and Dolto-Tolitch teach parents to use touch to play with the baby and even rock it while it is still inside the mother's body. This three-way connection confirms their emotional relationship and strengthens their sense of security. In Catherine Dolto-Tolitch's lovely words, "It opens the heart, which changes everything."

We do not yet have scientific proof that the fetus can store memories during its life in utero. However, it is reasonable to believe that it has a wide range of feelings and that these sensations must be recorded in its brain. "If only the baby could remember!" Dominique Simonnet writes.[4] "If only he could describe his metamorphoses, the swarming of cells deep within his tissues, if he could explain what he felt, remember the birth of life. But the first nine months of his existence will remain in the shadows of his memory. When he comes into the light, he will lose all memory of his stay deep within the uterine cave." However, at that moment he will be able to meet his mother in the outside world. They will meet, skin to skin, in their first physical contact, as well as when they look at each other, which both, probably, have been waiting to do.

"When a baby is born, he cries to breathe and then opens his eyes," pediatrician Edwige Antier explained at the French sixth annual conference on maternal psychology. "His gaze is very strange and deep as he seeks his identity because he does not know who he is. The baby is lost in this huge universe as if in a deep fog. He will come to life when he meets his mother's gaze, which will create an intense emotion and transmit her intelligence. At birth, intelligence is entirely emotional. That gaze is as important as oxygen . . . Looking into the mother's eyes is to come alive and exist in the world."

I share Dr. Antier's view. The intense emotion born of this gaze will be engraved in the brain as a primordial point of reference. We will seek it, cultivate it and bring it to life throughout infancy and early childhood. The desire to be loved is so powerful! That intense emotion will follow us into adult life and will return, happily or sadly, when we allow ourselves to remember what we experienced in childhood.

In the months that follow, the baby experiences a range of feelings related to her mother. Little by little, she "constructs" her mother and herself. The process begins through a symbiotic relationship with the mother and gradually becomes increasingly independent of her image. This period corresponds to what Jacques Lacan calls the mirror phase, when the baby acquires a perception of bodily physical unity. At around eighteen months, she becomes aware that she is separate from her mother but needs her. Later, at around two and a half, she will recognize herself in the mirror. The individuation process is liberating, but the trace of the symbiotic relationship remains with her forever. As she grows up, this daily relationship, composed of exchanges and experiences, continues to influence her life and sometimes even her destiny.

THE FATHER-CHILD DYAD

The father's role has long been considered marginal, limited to tolerating the mother's moods and tending to her every whim. If he shows interest is what is occurring inside her belly, the tone is more that of a playful observer ("Wow, hey, something's moving in there!") than informed father.

While it has become trendy for fathers to attend the child's birth, many doctors and parents still underestimate his role. He too is an important Other, in his own way. While he may not have a say in the matter for nine months, his voice is still heard. Observations made by Veldman and Dolto-Tolitch about the relationship between the father and baby in utero show how alive, active and responsive the fetus is. Psychoanalyst Didier Dumas is also interested in this issue. "Whether the father strokes his wife's belly or talks to the baby, the fetus senses the contact via the vibrations produced by the caress or voice even before it has a functioning auditory system." Dumas believes that the fetus hears the father's voice and even seeks it out, which is why haptonomy considers the father's active participation in—not just his attendance at—the birth to be so important.[5]

The father's role clearly extends beyond waiting on Her Ladyship hand and foot during the delicate period of pregnancy. We now recognize the father's importance, although some do not yet acknowledge it fully. The father supports the mother throughout pregnancy and takes responsibility for his part of the relationship, during the intrauterine period and after birth. He is not the second in command but a Lacanian co-great Other. This emotional triad is critical because it involves the father more directly than ever before in the pregnancy, the child's birth, its sense of security and its life. By giving the father a more direct role, we may now dare to think—and say—that excluding him risks confining the child in a potentially "stifling" bilateral relationship with the mother. The "new" father is thus not merely a trend that a few popular psychology magazines have cooked up as a catchy angle, but a significant sociological and psychological development whose impacts can be felt in the collective consciousness.

THE MOTHER-FATHER-CHILD TRIAD

Mother-child and father-child relationships are complex. Creating a three-way dynamic is no simple matter, either. Interpersonal relationships established against the backdrop of family also give rise to limitations, resistance and problems, in addition to the restrictive roles that society automatically assigns each individual.

Unfairness Weighs on the Mother

While the woman is happy that the child has a father and that she can offer an image of a unified family to the world, she often responds ambiguously when he demands his rightful place. Why should he enjoy that privilege, when all he did was support the pregnancy? Did he bear the child? Did he experience the discomforts, large and small? Did he feel the fear and pain of childbirth? And now that the benefits are kicking in, he wants to share them equally? But let's be honest. We don't usually put it in those terms. The mother assumes de facto responsibility for the essential aspects of the relationship with the baby (at least she knows what needs to be done). Both irritated and reassured to be consigned to the sidelines, the father contents himself with handling day-to-day operations. And since there's a thin line between contentment and delight, he'll be happy to cross it. The less that's asked of him, the happier he is, leading French psychoanalyst Christiane Olivier to write, "It often appears that the woman is as determined to claim responsibility for the child as the man is to avoid doing so."[6]

The Father Is Frustrated Too

Even if the man is happy and proud to become a father, he may find it difficult to accept the changed situation. Previously he enjoyed exclusive access to his wife and did not have to compete for her time. Now he has to share both with the newborn. Of course, most men would challenge that statement. Although it's not easy to accept that you could be jealous of your own child,

that's often the case. In the father's experience, the baby inter-
cepts and diverts the attention he used to enjoy. He quickly con-
nects the need to care for a tiny infant to his wife's loss of interest
in him, which is enough for him to feel abandoned, particularly
if the woman is overinvested in the relationship with the child,
whether to compensate for the anxiety associated with her new
maternal responsibilities or give free rein to her love for her baby.
In addition, he can no longer go out when he wants, be spontaneous, make love how, when or where he chooses or hang out
with his buddies. And he has to come home at a reasonable hour.
All these collateral frustrations can result in an abandoned, frustrated and jealous individual who is ready to resign.

Every Child Is an Oedipus

The child bears the considerable weight of parental and family
influences, pressures and projections, whether expressed
through love, affection and tenderness or feelings of frustration,
injustice or rivalry. These operate at both the conscious level (you
don't need to refer to the unconscious to know when the mother
is throwing a fit or the father is sulking, and vice versa) and the
unconscious level. (What is being said and if unsaid, heard
nonetheless? How does the child's unconscious hear and interpret the spoken and unspoken remarks?)

Psychoanalysis teaches us that the child passes through
various phases beginning at birth: oral, oral-sadistic, anal, anal-
sadistic, phallic, latency and genital. Each marks the child's development from birth through puberty. The phallic phase, which

occurs between three and five years of age, most directly concerns the mother-father-child triad. Doctrines differ as to its meaning. Freud believed that little boys develop "penis pride," and little girls, "penis envy," during this time. Later, others rejected such a specifically anatomical characterization, proposing that it involves belief in a symbol of power that psychologists call "the phallus," corresponding to the "penis fantasy" rather than the penis itself. Nonetheless, Freud believed that what he called the Oedipus complex emerges at the end of the phallic phase, when the child becomes attracted to the parent of the opposite sex and develops a jealous hostility toward the parent of the same sex. The little boy identifies with the father but fears him because he experiences the man as powerful and capable of castrating him. The father prevents the child from realizing his sexual desires (the prohibition against incest). The little girl falls in love with the father and sees her mother as a rival, but does not experience castration anxiety because she thinks that she does not have genitals.

Psychoanalyst Juan David Nasio takes another approach, which I find interesting. In an article on the "indispensable" Oedipus myth discussing the castration complex in girls, he explains that the phallus is not the penis, but the name given to the fantasy of the penis. "Everyone has the phallus, girls as well as boys," he writes. Any fantasy object with high emotional value can play that role—penis, clitoris, father, mother, house or even a career.[7] Nasio's notion diverges from Freud's here. Freud believes that the little girl's castration complex is triggered when she notices that the boy has a penis, while she does not. Nasio does not think that the lack of a penis on her body is significant, but rather her sense that she is missing "the physical reality confirming that she possesses the power of the phallus. She does not want the penis, but that which would make it possible to support its illusion."[8] This absence is the source of disillusionment, nostalgia and bitterness with respect to the mother, who has not prepared her for the loss of that illusion. While boys experience castration anxiety, girls' anxiety has to do with "losing the love of the object loved."[9]

As you can see, the love of each parent for the child and that of the child for the parents involve twists and turns. The roads leading there are full of promise but the route is mysterious and marked with obstacles. Seen from here, the undertaking resembles a rite of passage and the way forward, a route of passage. This route will lead us toward the self we will construct, enabling us to structure and define ourselves as individuals. Simultaneously, it will also guide us toward a life in the larger world, since the goal of all these experiences and trials is to forge individuals who can live as adults and participate in community life.

SIBLINGS PLAY A ROLE IN THE CHILD'S LIFE AND MEMORIES

Siblings compose the second important group of intrafamilial relationships. Sibling-related memories speak to the richness of interactions within the family and are thus part of the basic information I am particularly interested in when I ask an individual about his early childhood memories. If you are an only child, you may find this irrelevant, but we need to pause here.

The position we held in the family plays an important role in determining our perception of childhood and the childhood memories we retain. Perception of the world varies dramatically based on whether you were an only child, older or younger, boy or girl, big brother or little sister. Nearly every human trait is revealed in sibling relationships—from the noblest sentiments to the basest, from tender attachments to fierce competition, from loyalty to treachery. We all know the Bible story of Cain and Abel, in which Cain became furious when God preferred his brother's gift and, as you probably remember, Cain killed his brother. Fortunately, sibling relationships rarely end so tragically. Still, every parent with two or more children has witnessed at least one episode in which one child would have happily done away with another. We do our best to treat our children fairly and raise them in a spirit of harmony, but their differences always emerge, provoking conflict and misunderstanding. The pendulum of sibling relationships swings between differences on one side and feelings on the other.

Sibling Differences Complicate Life

A mother's heart swells to embrace all her children but does not divide its love. Unfortunately, her children don't behave in a similarly positive way. Tensions arising from their differences complicate their coexistence and create conflicts among them.

- Gender differences, which involve the full range of oedipal involvements (girls toward fathers, boys toward mothers), also play a role in how boys and girls perceive life. Parents' social and religious beliefs and how they choose to educate their children also reflect these differences. The notion that parents can raise boys and girls in a "gender-neutral" way is illusory; even if it were possible, the child's school and social environment would inculcate those differences.

- Age differences result in varying levels of maturity and thus varying opportunities. Younger children feel inferior and restrained, older ones feel shackled and they all feel that they've been treated unfairly.

- Interests vary too. Younger children always want to participate in older siblings' activities. The latter are unwilling to share their prerogatives because if everyone has the same rights, the privilege is meaningless.

- Finally, personalities differ. Character is a marvel of human chemistry, blending our genetic heritage, markers specific to our position in the sibling order and the family constellation, our physical and mental constitution, our upbringing, how we look at life and, finally, what life has in store for us.

These differences produce a range of affects, including negative feelings like jealousy, rivalry, competition, selfishness and a tendency to boast, which affect our relationships and are reflected in our memories.

Feelings for Siblings

Fortunately, the finest human feelings also flourish in sibling relationships. A child may often seek the understanding, tenderness, affection, admiration, rapport and support from an older brother or sister that parents, busy with their own existential or psychological problems, do not always have the time, leisure or ability to provide. Being brother and sister (or brother and brother or sister and sister) means being together almost all the time, especially if siblings share a bedroom. Childhood memories are full of moments together. These are intimate relationships built on common experiences, discoveries, secrets and confidences, as well as afternoons of aimless wandering and games in which make-believe princes and princesses put their courage to the test. Siblings may find each other exasperating, but not for lack of love. Rather, it's because they lack perspective, as they are privileged—and forced—to be intimate witnesses to each other's lives. As children and adults, we sometimes need to distance ourselves to come back.

Childhood memories of brothers and sisters not only reveal the kind of relationships an individual established with siblings, but are valuable indicators of the family atmosphere and the alliances and antagonisms among its members.

THE ROLE OF GRANDPARENTS AND EXTENDED FAMILY IN THE CHILD'S LIFE AND MEMORIES

Grandparents and extended family members (including uncles, aunts, nephews, nieces and cousins) make up the third and last major group of intrafamilial relationships.[10] These memories are usually tender and close, although they may also reflect strictness and harshness.

The memories I hear about time spent with grandparents often describe special moments that leave a lifelong imprint. My grandparents died before I was born, so I always admired and envied friends whose grandparents were still alive. Whether the older people lived nearby or far away, they always seemed to know just what the grandchildren needed. They were certainly popular! Children have a great time with grandparents, who tolerate almost any kind of behavior. You can cheat, break the rules, play the clown and be naughty but you know that they'll love you just the same. To them, even your faults are qualities. They don't watch or listen to you as much as drink you in.[11] Memories of activities and times with grandparents constitute unique stabilizing and calming elements in the child's emotional world, particularly if parents are absent, indifferent or withdrawn. (I refer to grandparents here, but the same could apply to any member of the extended family with whom the individual had a particularly close relationship.)

However, some grandparents fail to understand their role, demonstrating pettiness, arbitrariness, unfairness and betrayal, especially when they cannot avoid playing favorites among grandchildren. What a sad picture—grandparents who cannot open their arms to the unconditional love that all children are ready to give the people close to them. I'd prefer to think that this is the exception that proves the rule.

Grandparents almost always appear in childhood memories at some point. They also speak to the balance in relationships and the feeling of community that the individual has developed.

CHILDREN OF RECONSTITUTED FAMILIES

Although reconstituted families are not part of the classic close or extended family, I want to consider those relationships because they often mark our memories. When the host parent or his or her children behave cruelly or arbitrarily or play favorites, their actions may leave signs of sadness and pain. However, when the right seeds have been planted, often at a very young age, that wonderful and fertile ground can produce a respectful and loving family atmosphere. When that happens, the quality of memories from classic and reconstituted families does not differ fundamentally because, once again, they always reveal the spirit of the child within us. These are not second-class memories.

Of course every family situation is different. Some of you may have grown up in a family that was reconstituted after the death of a parent; others, following separation or divorce. Some have been part of a reconstituted family from a very young age and others from puberty. Some have learned to live with brothers and sisters who were not biological siblings, while others retained only-child status because the stepparent had no children of his or her own.

Whatever your situation, if you lived in a reconstituted family, your sensibility and personality determined how you experienced it. That's what counts.

Lya Luft was right. Childhood is indeed the ground we walk on throughout life. It bears the footprint of all the feelings, emotions and changes we have experienced from birth. Childhood is our ground and our memories are its paving stones. Sometimes the surface is smooth and flat, but it can be slippery, uneven, bumpy and nearly impassable. That's what our memories tell us. But how do they do that?

Part Three

*How to Read and Interpret
Childhood Memories*

CHAPTER 5

Mother-Father-Child Core Nuclear Relationships in Memories

Let us never forget that the meaning of
things heard is often revealed only later.
—SIGMUND FREUD, PSYCHOANALYTIC TECHNIQUE

TELL ME SOMETHING ABOUT YOUR LIFE YOU'VE NEVER TOLD ANYONE

When I was living in Berlin, I enjoyed playing the investigative reporter with friends and acquaintances. I would ask them, point-blank, to recount an incident they had never told anyone. The question was somewhat disconcerting because you don't quite know what to say when you're caught off guard. At the same time, I was always surprised to see how easily people would share their past when offered the chance, once the surprise passed. What began as a joke almost always ended as a deep and fascinating conversation about a life experience. Talking about our memories also allows us to use superlatives without being accused of pride, which is no small thing. Since we're dealing with ancient history, it's acceptable.[1]

AN UNUSUAL SELECTIVE SITUATION

When you ask about childhood memories, specifically from early childhood, the individual confronts an extremely unusual selective situation:

- First, the memories that come to mind spontaneously when we let our thoughts wander differ considerably from those we seek out intentionally when someone asks us for a memory.

In the former situation the conscious filters the memories because you have had time to reflect, sort and select certain ones. In the latter, the face-to-face encounter with the other person dominates and the unconscious will usually seek out the memories.[2] You may be wondering, then, about the value of the experiment I asked you to perform dealing with your own memories. In that situation, we're somewhere between the two—you are not completely alone, letting your thoughts wander, nor are you sitting face-to-face with me. If you followed the instructions and wrote down your memories spontaneously, your unconscious dictated them for the most part. However, if you tried to control things, your conscious stepped in and the interpretation of your memories will be somewhat limited.

- Second, a perceptual difference exists between wandering alone among your memories and being questioned by someone. Do you remember my story about the French national anthem? If I hum it to myself while I'm busy doing nothing, the words come into my head naturally. However, if someone asks me to sing the first stanza, especially if that person represents authority—and someone wielding a microphone most assuredly represents a form of authority—I'll be confused because my emotions will come into play. We face a similar situation when someone asks us for a childhood memory. The question creates a moment of relationship that places us in an intersubjective state and thus in a form of dependency (I am aware that you expect something from me).
- Third, an aspect of hypnotic suggestion underlies the request. If I ask someone for a memory, I assume the position of interrogator and place the other person in the position of interrogation subject, creating a climate of suggestion. The word "childhood" reinforces the hypnotic process because it evokes specific feelings based on our senses, sensations, emotions, and affective thoughts.

The combined effect of these three conditions points us to the most powerful influence in our distant past—the relationships we experienced and developed during infancy and childhood, particularly the relationship with our mother and father.

THE MOTHER-FATHER-CHILD
NUCLEAR RELATIONSHIP PRINCIPLE
(THE CORE NUCLEAR RELATIONSHIP PRINCIPLE)

In the classic case, when you ask someone to recount his or her early childhood memories, the individual first seeks those related to the mother-child dyad, then the father-child dyad, and last to sibling relationships. I call this the core or classic nuclear relationship principle. Later it will broaden to include the extended family (uncles, aunts, cousins, godparents and grandparents) and then to relationships with nonfamily members (from neighbors to shop owners, bus drivers and the school principal). As the child matures, these relationships expand gradually to the entire community of which he is a part, his social and religious community and ultimately the outside world.

Core nuclear relationships may appear in memories in conventional order (mother, father, siblings), randomly (siblings, father, mother) or not at all, as illustrated below. (For emphasis, I identify the family member involved in italics.)

Memories That Appear in Order

This example involves Anne, a twenty-five-year-old woman whose memories are presented in classic order (mother, father, sister).

First memory: When I was three, my *mother* mounted a little seat for me on her bicycle and took me with her to the grocery store.

Second memory: I was eight and I saw my *father*. He was responsible for security at the church. A circus had set up across the street. I am standing at the church entrance.

Third memory: I was three years old. We took my *sister* to kindergarten and I had a tantrum because I wanted to go too, but I wasn't old enough.

This illustrates a classic case of memory development.

Memories That Do Not Appear in Order

This involves a young man between twenty and twenty-five.

First memory: I was five or six. I was playing with *my brother* on the playground. He is two years older than I. We were arguing across the wall.

Second memory: I was almost four. I was terrified of shots. *My mother* took me to the doctor's office. I remember the street.

Third memory: I don't know how old I was, but I am standing in my cage bed [he meant to say crib but instead used this odd phrase]. It's morning and I'm waiting for *someone* to come get me. I'm trying to get out by myself too.

In this example, the brother appears first, followed by the mother, and then "someone," who could be either the mother or the father.

Memories in Which the
Classic Form Is Not Present

This involves a man in his thirties.

First memory: We were in Brittany. I was about seven and I was playing cops and robbers with a *friend*. I was always the policeman and I always lost the game. I don't know why.

Second memory: I was in Cannes. It was raining and *a woman* was taking care of me. She took me to visit a friend of hers.

Third memory: *At my grandmother's* house in Paris, all the bedrooms opened onto the patio. *My little sister* had a very quick temper. She was pounding on the floor. My grandmother grabbed her by the scruff of her neck and shut her in her room, but my sister came back out and resumed her tantrum in the living room.

Neither mother nor father appears in this series. The first memory involves a friend; the second, a woman; and the third, the grandmother and little sister.

We can say that the woman who recounted the first series of memories had a *classic* childhood and that, to a certain extent, her present life reflects it. Let me explain. Although men's and women's roles have shifted considerably in our era, the emotional and nourishing dimension is still strongly associated with the mother's image. She carries the child inside her body, where it grows and develops, and she is responsible for nourishing the child and providing most of his care. You may find this portrait conventional and stereotyped, but just flip through the ads in today's parenting magazines and you'll recognize that it still holds. The father's image is associated with protection and safety. Traditionally, he is responsible for maintaining order and defending the family from danger. The mother mediates the internal world; the father, the external. The mother symbolizes affection and the nourishing entity, while the father symbolizes protection and the law. The roles assigned each parent thus do not necessarily constitute reality, but a fantasized vision of their role.

When an individual makes successive references to the mother and father in one of the three childhood memories, we can conclude that they played an important role in his life (however you choose to understand the word "important"). The memory may be positive or comforting ("My mother mounted a little seat for me on her bicycle") or negative or painful ("My mother took me to the doctor for shots, which terrified me"). We must not jump to conclusions (if this, therefore that) when we listen to memories. There are no hard-and-fast "therefores" when it comes to interpreting them. We must be prepared to revise our interpretation at any moment if a new piece of information shifts the focus.

If parents do not appear, as in the third series of memories, their absence should not be interpreted as a sign of disaster, psychological problems or major difficulties. This is simply a piece of information that may reveal a known, long-standing conflict ("My mother and I were never very close") or an unsuspected one ("Even so, I have a wonderful relationship with both my parents") and should always be correlated with other information. Do you remember the three memories from my childhood? The first involved neither my mother or father, but rather a garden and a butterfly net. The second referred to my brothers and sisters. My mother did not appear until the third. I'll come back to that.

Finally, parents may be represented symbolically. For example, the house may symbolize the mother's belly, food or the nourishing breast. When we ask for an early childhood memory, we touch the emotions related to the mother's tenderness ("There's nothing like a mother's love") and the father's protectiveness ("My father is the strongest man in the world").

CORINNE DOESN'T UNDERSTAND WHY SHE
ALWAYS BREAKS OFF RELATIONSHIPS WITH MEN

Corinne came to see me because she had a problem with men. Several weeks into a relationship, her behavior would become intolerable and she would dump the man. She wanted to know why. She was startled when I asked her for an early childhood memory.

"Gosh, I hardly have any," she said. After thinking for a moment, she said, "I do have one. I am about five years old. I am in an apartment. I live there alone with my mother. We lived alone. She was dancing with me. We were wild, going around in circles."

"A second one?"

She paused, looking at me as if trying to figure out where I was heading.

"I'm around six. There's a bathtub. We're in that same apartment, giving my little brother a bath. I am six years older than he. We take him out of the tub and wrap him up. It was a sweet moment."

"And a third?"

"We're with my stepfather's family. There's a house with animals. I don't know why, but in this memory, I feel close to him there. I remember the image of riding on his back, holding on to his shoulders."

At first glance, the core nuclear relationships in Corinne's memories seem to be well established. In the first memory, we see an apartment (a nest) and a mother (love) who dances with her (the playful, active side of life). The scene conveys emotional security and nourishment.

The second portrays another intimate moment shared with her mother and baby brother. They are washing, drying and swaddling. Together, they are playing mommy and baby in a scene expressing the security and calm the mother provides. The father does not appear, but given the reason Corinne is seeing a therapist, we could have guessed that. Still, we wonder where he is.

The third memory reveals that Corinne has a stepfather, which, at first glance, suggests that her birth father is absent. However, this is a positive memory conveying closeness and tenderness. (What emerges from Corinne's personality corresponds to what she expresses in her memories. She is an attractive young woman, dark-haired, thin, almost angular, with very fine features and a musical, slightly drawling voice.) At the same time, Corinne says, "I don't know why, but I felt close to him there." You don't have to be a Sherlock Holmes to guess that this was probably one of the rare (perhaps only) times when she felt that closeness. Why didn't she have a stronger commitment to the relationship? At our next meeting, I learned that she did not meet her birth father until she was fourteen, following an episode in which she ran away with a girlfriend. He'd always lived in the same area but existed in the shadows of her life. "I had trouble accepting certain things," she told me. "Beginning in preadolescence, I was extremely unhappy but for no reason." Maybe there was a reason, after all. Corinne told me that she had imagined so much—if only about her absent father—but no one ever told her the truth. She felt different and unloved, as if she didn't belong to the family and had disappointed everyone. She retained that self-image into adulthood and behaved in such a way that it actually became true.

I believe that because no one ever told Corinne that her father was nearby, she was waiting for him unconsciously, while at the same time rejecting her stepfather. She could not make attachments with men and broke off relationships because she had not invested in the oedipal father-daughter relationship and thus had no point of reference for a long-term one. She knew how to play mommy and baby, but did not know how to be a woman with a man. As is often the case in this kind of session, those three childhood memories brought us straight to the heart of Corinne's problem and allowed us to express it clearly and understandably.

HENRY IS CRUEL TO OTHERS, ESPECIALLY WOMEN

For the past three months, Henry had been dating a young woman he'd met recently. He'd come to see me because he did not want to make the same mistakes he made with his wife. They were divorced two years ago. He was aware that he had a somewhat aggressive attitude toward other people, especially women and particularly the woman who shared his life. He told me that to assert himself, he would put other people down and treat them as inferior. "It's not very appealing behavior," he said. "It's even slightly sadistic." He wanted to understand the reason for this failing. After he explained some additional problems (with his children), I asked him to tell me a memory.

The following incident occurred when he was between eight and twelve, so it was not his first memory.

"I was fighting with my brother. We were in the living room. I got him in a judo throw and sent him flying, but he wasn't hurt."

When I asked him for a second memory, he said, "I loved miniature cars. Every time my parents took a trip, they would bring one home for me. Actually, my father was the one who would bring them. My father brought them back."

"And a third memory?"

"We always had a housekeeper even though my mother hadn't worked for a long time. My father was very present in the family. I would go to him, not my mother, when I needed something."

Just in case, I asked him for a fourth.

"I am three or four years old and I'm sitting in my high chair. The housekeeper was there. I can see the kitchen. She turned around and I pulled on the string to undo her apron."

As you note, the classic order of memories is reversed here. The brother appears first; next, the father (who is very warm); and then the mother (who does not appear to be very tender). Given what he said about his mother, that's not unexpected. The housekeeper appears last.

Henry is quite a fighter. The two brothers were clearly rivals. The next session confirmed that assessment, when Henry explained that he and his brother had been working together for twenty years. Given the situation, it's easy to see that getting his brother in a good judo hold would certainly make it clear who's who. Henry didn't want to harm his brother ("He wasn't hurt"), but to make clear that he was in charge. I might well think that the same dynamic could play a role in his relationships with others.

The father appears in the second memory. He seems to fulfill his responsibilities well, perhaps including even maternal ones.

"I would go to him, not to my mother," Henry added to the account of his third memory. Henry's father is an interesting fellow. Think about all those little cars he'd bring back from trips. You could say that Henry bears a grudge against his mother. Twice he said, "My father brought the little cars back," suggesting that his mother probably wouldn't have taken the trouble to make him happy in that way. So far, we've got the brother/rival, the beloved father and the slightly suspect mother. The third memory confirms the suspicion immediately. Henry doesn't mince words on this subject. "My mother exaggerated," he said. "She didn't have anything to do all day long, but my father had to pay a housekeeper to look after the house and take care of us. So I gave my mother the cold shoulder. When I needed something, I went to my father, never to her."

The classic oedipal process didn't gain much traction here. In psychoanalytic terms, we would say that the father corresponds to the good object and the mother, to the bad. She probably suffered for it and must have invested more heavily in the relationship with the little brother. Perhaps he was sweeter and more considerate and could deal with her more effectively. Henry agreed. From all appearances, his mother had always preferred the younger brother and still favored him, for example, by inviting him to dinner without his older brother.

Childhood situations profoundly mark an individual's life well into adulthood. Even if you are accustomed to this kind of situation and think you've tended carefully to the wound, forty years later you may still feel the pain of being considered second

best. A recurring feeling that someone else will always be preferred can create contradictory emotions, leading you to prevent
others from loving you by being disagreeable, insulting or cruel.
That's what Henry concluded. He needed to learn a different way
to relate to women—his own way. Why not? I don't see Henry in
therapy anymore, but I would like to know how he has changed.

The fourth memory, about the housekeeper, has a nourishing
aspect. When a child is in a high chair, it's usually because it's
time to eat. When the memory is set in the kitchen and the
housekeeper is present, we can assume that she is preparing food
and will feed the child. She appears here as a nourishing entity and
thus a good object. Henry probably experienced her as a substitute mother, so "playing with the string" (the cord) seems to
make sense.

CHAPTER 6

The Other Primary
Active Components
of Memories

Let each one examine his thoughts,
and he will find them all
occupied with the past and the future.
—BLAISE PASCAL, *THOUGHTS*

IN ADDITION TO memories of the father, mother and family constellation, most memories include people outside that circle, those related to time, place, objects and trauma, involving the senses and emotions and, last, relating directly to character.

MEMORIES OF PEOPLE OUTSIDE
THE FAMILY CONSTELLATION

Every person who plays a specific role in our life may have a place in our memories, from the postman to Marlon Brando in *The Godfather* to a friend.

I am not going to interpret the following memories, but they characterize the range of experiences that can leave a lasting mark in memories.

Florence: I was playing in the courtyard of our apartment building. I was three or four. A woman came out of the building and said to me, "Your mother is feeling blue." I imagined my mother reaching up to touch a wide blue sky.

Maryanne: I was at summer camp. I must have been around eight years old. Being Jewish, I did not attend mass, and neither did the other Jewish children. The others got dressed up, but we didn't. We had to wait for them before we could eat, so we pretended that we were at mass too.

Jack: There was a girl I liked a lot in sixth grade. It was the first time I'd noticed a girl. It was love at first sight. I was crazy about her.

Lydia: I was around eight years old. I had a neighbor, a little girl, who always kicked me. I was afraid of her.

Gerard: I was two years old. I was jumping around, doing tricks and showing off in front of the little girls. I scraped my face and had to go to the hospital. Still, it's a good memory.

John: I was seven, at camp. I enjoyed it a lot. I used to go during every school vacation. Later I became a camp counselor.

For the most part, these memories deal with situations or actions. The other individual's identity is less important than the incident involving him or her. Indeed, it is quite unusual to remember names many years later.

Everyone knows that remembering names can be difficult. How often have you said, "Oh, it's on the tip of my tongue!

What's that guy's name?" In 2004 a German magazine published an article describing an experiment dealing with what is known as the baker/Baker paradox.[1] A team of psychologists showed a group of volunteers a set of photographs of people identified by name (for example, Mr. Baker, Mr. Carpenter and Ms. Farmer) and asked the volunteers to memorize the names. They showed a second group the same photographs but identified the individuals by occupation (for example, baker, carpenter and farmer). Later, all the volunteers looked at the photographs again and were asked for each individual's identity. The volunteers from the first group found it difficult to remember the names, but the members of the second group had a much easier time remembering the subjects' occupations. The explanation is simple. A proper name means nothing in and of itself, but only characterizes the person who bears it. If I say, "My friend is named Carpenter," I'm not saying anything about him. However, if I say, "My friend *is* a carpenter," I provide a host of details about what he does, the kinds of tools he uses and the people he deals with. That makes the job of remembering much easier.

MEMORIES OF ANIMALS

As you might imagine, animals, particularly pets, play a large role in childhood memories. Did you have a dog or a cat when you were growing up? Was there a pet at your grandmother's house or at your uncle's place in the country? These memories are particularly touching because they refer not only to the animal but also to the atmosphere in which the experience took place. Many of you have wonderful memories of animals.

Animals play a key role because they mediate between humans and the natural environment. As society distances us further and further from our primal nature, it is useful to remember that before we became "neuronal man,"[2] we were hominid *Australopithecus,* with many traits and behaviors quite close to those of other animal species.[3] The family pet also has a unique, inexhaustible ability to accept human affection. Children and old people who have close relationships with a favorite animal understand this. An animal may function as therapist, as some people feel more at ease in the company of a pet than another human being. In such cases, the presence of a pet that plays a particularly important role may reveal a process of emotional compensation. The pet can help compensate for solitude, sadness, illness or fear of others. This will also be visible in the individual's memories. For example, if a person recounts three memories that all present a connection to his dog, you may reasonably conclude that the animal was his best friend and that his family group may have been lacking in some way.

Memories involving domestic animals are not always sweet. I remember being attacked by a wolfhound when I was a child. (I know "attacked" is a strong word.) I was running to meet my father's car when the dog jumped on me, although I think he was playing. Nonetheless, I was terrified, which is probably why I never wanted a dog in the house. In any event, we weren't "dog people" in our family. A young woman from Quebec told me an amusing story about an animal. One afternoon, her family was napping on the patio at their house when a caribou approached and made off with one of her father's sandals. Neither the caribou nor the sandal has been seen since! Another patient, Benjamin, described a serious incident that occurred when he was young. His parents had told him to stay indoors because the gardener was tending to a beehive. As usual, he disobeyed and ended up covered with bees. Surprisingly, he was not stung, which no one could understand.

Memories related to animals generally provide details about the individual's emotional life and level of sociability.

MEMORIES OF PLACE

We have many memories of place and almost everyone has them. They help us establish the context of the memory and function as a memory aid, or mnemonic device, as we say in psychology. Once the setting is established, the action follows.

The account of the memory often follows the description of a place. You will often hear someone say, I was at home. . . , In my room. . . , When I lived in New York. . . , When we lived abroad. . . , When I was in the hospital. . . , At my grandparents' house . . . or At school . . .

Here are several examples of place-based memories, transcribed directly from the speakers' words.

Amelia: *I was about six. I was always alone playing in the garden. In fact, we rarely left the house.*

Patricia: *When I was five, my mother locked me in the attic because my father was coming to tell her he wanted a divorce.*

John: *When I was seven, my brothers and sisters and I used to play in the apartment. We fought often.*

If you know how to listen and understand, places can offer a wealth of information. For example, phrases like "in the house," "where we lived," "at our place in the country," "at my grandmother's" or "in my room" clearly refer to living space, which includes a security-related dimension that I call "the mother's womb." "At school" and "at church" (or at the mosque or synagogue) tend to refer to the community. If a person is an immigrant and begins his sentence, "In Mexico," "In France" or "In China," he is referring to a past for which he still feels nostalgia.

THE ROLE OF TIME
IN MEMORIES

The past, or particular periods of life, can also help us reconstruct our memories, for example, "I remember when I was in the army," "When we lived in our first house," "Before we moved to Chicago," or "At the lake during summer vacation." Time is also a valuable mnemonic ally and serves as a point of reference. It's not unusual to hear someone say, "That couldn't have happened in Denver because we were still living in the big house."

Some people, like Michelle, anchor their memories strongly in time. She is a real *bon vivant* from Nice, in the south of France.

First memory: Every year, we used to go to the Fête des Mais (an ancient spring festival) in the garden of the monastery. My father set up a stand there.

Second memory: Every Thursday, I went to a remedial education class with one of the teachers.

Third memory: On Saturday afternoons, we went shopping at the supermarket.

Circumscribing memories within a defined time period and emphasizing stable points of reference help her maintain control over her life and limit her exposure to risk.

You will note that Michelle unconsciously chooses memories of events that occurred regularly and repeatedly. *Every year, every Thursday, on Saturday afternoons* are signposts that probably reassure her. Of course, if she worked in a watch repair shop, that would be the icing on the cake, but she runs a dry cleaning shop. Still, carrying that idea a bit further, a dry cleaner's could be linked to the seasons—as they change, we take our clothes to be cleaned before storing them for the next year.

MEMORIES OF OBJECTS AND THINGS

These are very unusual memories because they seem to shift space, time and relationships to others into the background. In my psychotherapy practice, when they are recalled first, I tend to see them as screen memories. (I discussed screen memories in the earlier section about Freud.) In general, gifts are the first objects we might expect to find in memories (anniversary, Christmas, retirement or birthday), but many unexpected ones appear.

Tom: *I was thirteen. It was 1963 and I remember the first television.*

Deborah: *I was four or five. I was playing with a can. I put my foot inside and walked around with it stuck to my foot. It made a clattering sound.*

Bernard: *I was three, lying on the ground playing with a little truck, or maybe it was a car.*

Cecilia: *I can see a huge eucalyptus tree, but I don't remember where it was.*

Notice how these memories are recounted in just a few words. People often say, "It's not really a memory, but more like a flashback or an image."

Such objects and things must have been extremely important. Perhaps they remained with the person throughout his life, whether as a memory or a thought. We all had a favorite object during childhood—an item of clothing, a special blanket or a good luck charm. You might have had a special relationship with it, especially if you were solitary or if events isolated you from other people. I recall Hugo Hamilton's reference to his mother in his memoir, *The Speckled People:* "My mother started writing in her diary every day because that's your only real friend for life."[4] The object might have been a diary, but it could also have been a doll, a book or even a piece of wood or a stone that, in your imagination, hailed from a far continent, stamped with the mark of history. For those who need them, inanimate objects have "a soul that attaches to our soul and the strength to love."[5]

MEMORIES THAT FEATURE
THE SENSES AND THE EMOTIONS

Memories featuring the senses and the emotions are very different. They may range from movement (ballet class) to smells (cotton candy), sights (fireworks), sounds (church bells) and mouth-watering tastes (grandmother's macaroni). They may also include horrible sights (a raccoon run over by a car) and disgusting experiences (my little brother, who made me lick the snot running out of his nose).

Mary: I was six. My mother had gone to England for a year, and we were at boarding school. I was in class when she came back. I didn't know that she was coming home. I was bursting with joy. I remember that I cried.

Robert: I was between four and six. My grandmother called me into the kitchen to taste the sauce she was cooking.

There are unpleasant memories too, of discomfort (an internal medical exam), injustice (a cruel teacher), abandonment (divorce) and violence (father beating the mother). They may also include traumatic recollections (memories of war) and poisonous memories (incest). We also have memories of regrets and the full range of guilt feelings that go along with them.

Jill: I was eleven or twelve. My mother was telling me about sex. I was in bed, in my room. The light was off. She was explaining that this was something very romantic that you did with a special person. I was so embarrassed.

André: I was around four or five. I remember that my mother hit my sister and pulled her hair.

Christine: My mother beat my older sister viciously throughout my entire childhood. I had to watch. She never raised a hand against me, and I never understood why.

Trauma-Related Memories

Childhood traumas (incest, physical and psychological abuse, abandonment, crime and accidents, as well as serious illness or the illness or death of a family member) are generally in the foreground of the memories that are recounted. They leave an indelible mark on the individual and probably shaped his way of life. We would describe them as "the most important event" in a person's life. Ordinarily, other people have no idea about them. I remember a young man, an only child, whose mother tried to commit suicide several times by taking an overdose of medication. One morning, finding her lying motionless in bed once again, he decided that he'd had enough, so he left her and went to school. This was a dual trauma for him. He experienced the horrible sight of his mother lying there unconscious, and his remarkably detached reaction left him feeling like a monster. He remembered that his mother recovered, although he no longer recalled the details.

However, childhood memories do not operate systematically. You might expect that if an individual suffered a traumatic experience, it would automatically appear in his first three memories, but that is not the case. This shows that childhood memories are dynamic, not static, and that they are more closely related to the person's current life situation than to his past. A young woman related the following series of three childhood memories. The first involved a bicycle ride; the second, an elderly woman who looked after her while her mother was at work; and the third, a move. While we were discussing them, the young woman stopped for a moment and said, "That's funny, there are two important memories that I've clearly buried." Without giving me a chance to ask more questions, she continued. "The first is a very bad car accident I was in with my parents. I had to spend several weeks in the hospital. The second has to do with some serious problems I have with one of my aunts, who hated me." I knew that at the time, this young woman's life was happy, full and open, so I was not surprised that she was able to repress such negative memories.

While traumatic memories may be extremely negative or painful, the brain does not appear to be governed by a "duty to remember," which is probably just as well. It keeps the traumatic experiences in order, so to speak, allowing the conscious and the unconscious to establish and maintain equilibrium—up to a certain point.

MEMORIES THAT RELATE TO CHARACTER

Memories can reveal a particular character type and often correspond to it. A person with a fearful nature will remember fear, apprehension and anxiety; an irritable person will recall disputes, conflicts or quarrels; a star who seeks adulation will have memories of remarkable adventures; and a rebel will recall transgressions and violations. However, the classification system is rarely so simple. Any three given memories are unlikely to correspond to three character-related situations. The personality tendency is more likely to be revealed in the blend of the three memories, although the following series of memories demonstrates that that is not always the case.

GABRIEL LETS HIMSELF BE SWEPT AWAY

Gabriel came to see me about a broad concern. He wasn't happy with the way he was living. Time seemed to be moving quickly, and everything was slipping away. I asked him about his childhood memories. He said he didn't have precise recollections from his childhood but rather flashbacks or memories of a certain mood. However, I found them to be quite specific and powerful.

First memory: I was five or six and we lived on a steep street that opened onto a little square. I had received a toy car as a birthday present. My mother told me to stay in the square and not go down the street. I disobeyed her. The car gathered speed and rolled over. I ended up with blood all over my face.

Second memory: I was four or five. A playmate was annoying me. I don't know what came over me, but I took a brick and threw it at his hand, breaking his wrist.

Third memory: I was about thirteen. My friend and I were riding bikes. He had wanted me to come with him that afternoon. I didn't really want to, but eventually I went. I fell and ended up scraped and bloody.

Aren't these memories of accidents surprising? From all appearances, Gabriel must have been an energetic kid and a daredevil. However, I think that the most important information lies elsewhere. The common denominator here is that Gabriel allowed himself to be swept away. In his first memory, speed carried him down that steep street; in the second, anger had serious consequences for his friend; and in the third, his friend carried him away ("I didn't want to, but eventually I went"), and we know the outcome. Gabriel appears to lack a personal framework that would allow him to take charge of his own life. Even these memories seem to escape him, as if they lacked substance. He describes them as mood memories, but they also lack a strong *I*. Outside forces seem to dominate him, and he appears to exercise little control.

Once decoded, these memories provided Gabriel a key to reading his own map and a compass to guide his reflection and help him take a new approach to the issues facing him.

The world of memories is mysterious. When you know how to decipher it, it is a wonderful world too. Now that you have these tools, I hope you have a clearer sense of the process. What about your own three memories? Have you identified any of the characteristics I've discussed in these chapters? Do your memories reflect the principle of core nuclear relationships or seem to ignore it? Is there a common thread among the three? Are they consistent with your present life? I assume that some of these issues are still a bit unclear, so I'm going to provide you another tool.

CHAPTER 7

Outwardly Directed
Movement in Memories

*The places that we have known belong not only to the
little world of space on which we map them for our
own convenience.*
—MARCEL PROUST, SWANN'S WAY

THE PRINCIPLE OF core nuclear relationships is just one of the
two key principles associated with the dynamic, living structure of memories. I call the other the principle of outwardly directed movement, or the voyage principle (I'll explain my choice
of words soon). To simplify matters, I'll refer to it as the "movement principle," or simply movement, but please remember that
it always implies movement toward the larger world, or from the
interior world toward the exterior world. Movement expresses all
aspects of "exteriority" (the outside material world) and may be

represented in memories by going on vacation, visiting another country, moving, taking the train or riding in a car. Sometimes the movement is not so easy to read. For example, it may be symbolized by a surfboard, a pair of roller skates you received as a gift when you were little or even—why not?—a shopping cart. It may sometimes involve blocked movement, as when a person says, "My parents refused to buy me a bicycle."

Many of the memories described in the previous chapter involved movement. Do you remember Michelle, the woman from Nice ("We *went* to the Fête des Mais," "We *went* to the pool," "We *went* to walk the dog")? Or Annie, and the little seat on her mother's *bicycle?* Or John, who loved to *go* to camp three times a year, not to mention Henry and his little *cars*. Yes, even toy cars can symbolize movement.

While core nuclear relationships provide information about the individual's protected internal emotional world, the movement principle sheds light on how he experiences the exploratory dimension of the outside world. We return here to the issue of the mother (mediator of the internal world) and father (mediator of the external world), first raised in Chapter 5. Psychologist Abraham Maslow has noted that "in the choice between giving up safety or giving up growth, safety will ordinarily win out."[1] Similarly, I would say that core nuclear relationships address the need for safety, and movement addresses the need for growth. Remember this formula: nuclear relationships = safety, movement = growth.

In general, every series of three memories includes an aspect of movement. If it does not appear to be present in the initial account, it will emerge when the individual provides additional details. Movement may appear in memories in different ways, and its interpretation will thus vary. It may be expressed clearly or symbolically and may be absent or blocked.

Let me qualify that statement right away. Memories that do not include movement do not indicate a major problem or disorder. As you grasp all the information that emerges from the three memories, you will be able to understand their specific meaning.

When Outwardly Directed Movement Is Expressed Clearly

There is not much to say about this kind of movement, except that it usually appears in every series of classic memories. A young woman told me, "I was three or four. I went to a friend's house, which was really far away. My sister searched for me everywhere. She was in a total panic. I laugh every time I think about it." This memory portrays a little adventurer who set off to explore the world and saw nothing wrong with her actions.

Ordinarily, movement appears in only one memory, although it may appear in all three and even several times in each one. Elise, an energetic, pretty young woman with a strong personality, recounted five memories. Each features movement.

First memory: My earliest memory is of riding a kick scooter. It had no brake, and I hurtled down a long steep street at top speed. My mother was afraid I would fall on the curves.

Second memory: We played leapfrog at my grandparents' house.

Third memory: We used to come home from kindergarten on the bus at the end of the day.

Fourth memory: I remember when I learned to ride a bike. My parents bought one with training wheels. After a few minutes, I told my father to take them off, and I managed to ride on my own right away.

Fifth memory: I remember that we moved a lot.

When I pointed out the distinctive nature of her memories, Elise said, laughing, "That doesn't surprise me. I love to travel. I guess I should apply for a job at the airport." That would suit her perfectly!

While I was working on this section, my son came home from school and stopped in to say hello. I wondered how movement appears in the memories of a fourteen-year-old, so I asked him. Thoughtful young man that he is, he sat down and began talking.

First memory: I'm in my crib, crying. You and mom came in. You picked me up, walked over to the window in the hall with me and said, "Look out here, look."

Second memory: We stayed in a hotel in Burgundy. I had my little plastic golf clubs and I was playing on the gravel path.

Third memory: I was with my friends. We got into our little cars and rode down the street.

Nothing unusual here. These are the kind of memories one would expect from a developing adolescent. He is obviously drawn to the external world, as his three memories include three examples of outwardly directed movement.

First memory: Core nuclear relationships are present. His mother and father (oops; his father and mother) are there. His father takes him to the window and points to something outside (I wanted to distract him from his unhappiness by drawing his attention to something else). By showing him the outside world through the window, I am the person who facilitates exteriority.[2] His mother is there too, standing next to me. Her presence reassures him and represents the emotional and nourishing dimension. Her role is to facilitate interiority.

Second memory: Heading toward Paris, we passed through Burgundy, placing us in the middle of a memory of movement. He is with his parents at a hotel, a substitute for the home. My son is safe and can play, knowing that he is secure. He says that he was playing golf outside (the external world).

Third memory: He and his friends (tendency to form social groups) go down the hill (the outside world) in their cars (symbolic movement). It would be difficult to find a more comprehensive example of a memory of movement.

Perhaps you wonder whether memories differ based on whether the child is a boy or girl. I believe the answer depends less on gender than on upbringing, character and style of life. If a little girl is brought up according to traditional norms (with dolls and tea parties), her memories may well reflect that. If she is raised as a tomboy, they will tell the opposite story.

I had some doubts as I reviewed the above paragraphs, so I asked a girl my son's age to tell me three memories from her early childhood.

First memory: I was visiting my grandmother with my parents. They bought me an ice cream cone shaped like a clown. The nose was made of chewing gum.

Second memory: We're in our apartment. My brother wasn't born yet. There was a swing hanging from the doorway to my room.

Third memory: We are in the same apartment. My mother and I hid in the bathroom when my father came home. My father walked in and said, "Is anyone here?" We yelled, "Boo!" He was really scared, and we all laughed.

The house appears in all three memories. The first includes an element of movement (the visit), but the first words are, "I was at my grandmother's." Core nuclear relationships are also present (parents, brother, grandmother, mother and father).

However, don't jump to the conclusion that girls' memories refer only to interiority and boys' feature only movement. Let me repeat: what counts is upbringing, not gender.

Movement provides important information for the interpretation of your memories because it illustrates how you understand the external world; whether you have a symbiotic, osmotic or contradictory relationship with your internal world; and what kind of connection and what degree of friction exists between your external and internal worlds. This information can help explain how you approach the world. Do you take an active or a passive stance? Do you act or react? Are you immobile?

To live is to act, as the saying goes. But based on what? And how? According to what plan? There are no easy answers to those questions. However, our memories, particularly those that include elements of outwardly directed movement, can offer insight into how we manage our lives.

BERTRAND FINDS IT DIFFICULT TO TAKE ACTION

Bertrand is a beaming, open young man with many fine qualities. He tells me that he senses ambiguity in his personality that he doesn't understand. He is an active person but feels that "something is preventing his life from moving forward." For example, he loves to travel and understands that it requires money, but he doesn't like to work. "I love the result, but not the process of getting from here to there. Sometimes, it's the reverse." He doesn't understand how to take action. This conflict has already caused him to fail in many areas, including his education. "I've abandoned my goals," he says. "I'm not lazy, but there is something holding me back—a fear or an inability to act, as if a brake were slowing me down." I turn the conversation to his childhood memories.

First memory: My mother is looking down at me from above.

Second memory: I'm at my grandmother's in Brittany. She killed chickens by cutting out their tongue and hanging them from a cord.

Third memory: I'm in an elevator. My mother slaps me. "That's for later," she says.

I questioned him about his mother's look. He found it difficult to talk about because he didn't want me to think badly of her. I explained that we weren't talking about his mother but about his interpretation, at a given moment, of a particular event in his past. He then explained that he would freeze when she looked at him (the memory of an impression). She had a negative outlook about everything. As soon as you chose to take even a small step, she would be there to warn you about all the awful possibilities. She was always discouraging and talked only about risks and dangers.

That memory alone helps to explain Bertrand's semifearful attitude toward life. A look that freezes can paralyze and a negative, pessimistic view of life can inhibit movement.

His second memory involves movement (to Brittany), as it is set at the house of his mother's mother. This memory suggests violent action but also reflects rural traditions common at that time. I suppose that cutting the chicken's tongue would prevent it from screeching and allow it to be bled cleanly. Even so, it is hardly a tender memory. This is one tough woman—a grandmother with the guts to grab a chicken, yank open its mouth and cut out its tongue. A child who sees a woman doing that must say to himself that this woman is capable of anything. Wouldn't a psychoanalyst see an act of castration somewhere in all this? Bertrand's memory expresses both movement (Brittany) and the accompanying danger that could prevent someone from moving, as if a gas pedal and a brake were operating simultaneously and at cross-purposes.

The third memory involves movement (the elevator), but also refers to confinement in a closed space, offering another example of both an action and a brake on action.[3]

Bertrand's three memories have a dynamic/static texture. Movement is present, but action is blocked. The mother's negative look freezes, creating a sense of dread at the prospect of action. The grandmother kills chickens that would prefer to continue living and "tortures" and hangs them. The elevator represents movement but also confinement. In combination, this suggests an individual whose style of life is open to action but who is blocked from acting. Interestingly, these three memories operate in the vertical plane: the mother's look from above, the chickens suspended overhead, and the elevator that travels vertically (until proven otherwise). In Bertrand's relationship with his mother, one person was clearly "above" and the other "below." In other words, this is a dominant/submissive relationship. Finally, the father, who usually introduces the child to the external world, is strangely absent.

WHEN OUTWARDLY DIRECTED MOVEMENT APPEARS IN SYMBOLIC FORM

Memories of symbolic movement are found primarily in children's games. Examples include playing airplane, leapfrog (as we saw in Elise's memory) and cars (Henry and his father). Movement may also be symbolized by a horse-drawn carriage, a bathtub toy or a miniature musical merry-go-round (kitschy, I know).

Memories involving sports also reveal varying degrees of symbolic displacement. The sport chosen also provides useful information on the person's attitude toward life, whether active, passive or reactive. For example, mountain climbing, golf and squash are dramatically different activities.

Symbolic displacement can be more difficult to identify. One of Julian's memories involved freeing a bird from its cage. "Why did you let it go?" his mother asked. "I didn't want to see it in a cage," he answered. Guess what he does for a living? He works for the national railroad system. Some forms of expression may suggest movement, but they can be subtle and should be handled carefully. This reminds me of a man whose account of his memories began, "When I was little, it was amazing how the smell of tennis balls just carried me away." Indeed, that kind of "transport" can also symbolize movement.

The intensity of the movement, and thus the need for exteriority, is directly proportional to the symbol's coding. If the movement appears symbolically and is not immediately recognizable, that is because the unconscious wants to define its contours and nuances.

Seeking an interpretation is useful, but I caution against struggling to find a symbol where none exists or none is needed. We should not fall into the trap of searching for something when we no longer know what we are looking for or why. "Some ruses are so subtle that they defeat themselves," Kafka warned in "The Burrow."[4] The same is true when it comes to analyzing memories.

WHEN OUTWARDLY DIRECTED MOVEMENT IS ABSENT FROM MEMORIES

Memories without features of movement are rare. The very nature of life requires a certain geographic mobility. When movement does not appear in the three-memory series, this raises the question of whether the individual spent her childhood in a confined or symbiotic milieu and whether parents and teachers communicated an arm's-length (don't bother other people) or fearful (beware of other people) view of the world. If the analysis of the three memories reveals that the child's life was focused primarily on the home and family circle, we may conclude that the individual acquired a pessimistic or anxious view of the external world during childhood.

I had to search long and hard in my archives for a series of memories that do not include an element of movement. (In the course of that research, I noted that memories of vacations and scenes with grandparents appear more frequently than others.) Ten years ago, a woman who lived on Reunion Island, a French island in the Indian Ocean, told me the following series of memories. (I offer that geographic detail because I believe that insularity can contribute to a feeling of confinement, which could explain why movement is absent from these three memories, although I don't think that was the case here.)

Marie-Claire, twenty-two, began crying as soon as she walked into my office. She had an imploring expression, as if she were waiting for me to take charge. The conversation was awkward, and I had a hard time getting her to explain why she was there. How had this young woman landed in my office? As it turned out, she had come to France to study judo. Sensing her extreme reserve and seeing her physical discomfort during class, the instructor suspected a serious problem. He recommended that she see a psychologist, thinking therapy might help her open up.

Marie-Claire was lovely. She carried herself with grace and distinction, but she also had an absent air. Because she found it so difficult to speak about the present, I thought she might be more comfortable discussing the past. I asked her to tell me three childhood memories in succession. She didn't pour out a saga but did become a bit more communicative.

First memory: I was at home and I heard laughter. My cousin was talking on the phone, trying to convince a girl to go out with him. My brother and sister were there and they were teasing him. I felt bad for my cousin.

Second memory: Again, I'm at home. I pulled my sister's hair and she hit me hard in the stomach.

Third memory: I was trying on my new judo uniform with my mother. My brother was playing around and poked me. My mother slapped him.

You probably noticed that these three memories are all set within the confines of the house. Family life (cousin, brother, sister, mother) clearly occupies an important place, and the external world has a minimal presence. This family's life feels shuttered and closed off, and violence seems to have a place there, although limited to a few slaps. Could it be a form of communication within this family? Last, as is often the case with such memories, the father is conspicuously absent. That makes sense, as he would generally be the person to convey exteriority.

As we interpreted her memories together, Marie-Claire confirmed my analysis. Yes, she lived an isolated life. "Closed up like an oyster," she said. But she wasn't always like that. As a little girl, she was very open and reached out to everyone. She withdrew when she entered adolescence or, rather, when she started menstruating, at around twelve. She thought it was important not to attract attention anymore. She had become a woman, although she still felt like a little girl. In her personal relationships, she had always been afraid of her brother, who behaved like a tyrant. She was ashamed of being afraid. To flee the fear of others, she had closed herself off in her own world but could no longer tolerate that way of life. She was tremendously grateful to her judo instructor for prompting her to take this step and hoped things would finally change. I can't recount the full story because this is neither the time nor place, but life did change dramatically for her, starting with her relationship with her brother. She refused to accept his behavior any longer, which gave her tremendous comfort as her continuing sense of shame gave way to a (still slight) feeling of pride.

Sometimes a path that appears to be blocked forever opens up, allowing us to make a fresh start. When Marie-Claire returned to Reunion Island, I recommended that she continue working with a psychologist there.

WHEN OUTWARDLY DIRECTED MOVEMENT IS BLOCKED

As in life, the variations and shadings of memories mean that things are never as permanent and unchanging as we might think. No sooner do we come up with a rule for a given situation, than the first exception breaks it. This phenomenon is particularly evident in dealing with memories of movement. Our analysis will provide tremendous insights into the underlying psychology if we approach the process cautiously and carefully.

Our attitude toward life may be expressed by a desire for action, boldness, freedom, discovery and adventure. It may also be expressed by a need for reliable signposts, carefully marked paths and safety zones.

In memories of blocked movement, we find this ambiguity dating back to early childhood between the desire for growth and security, between curiosity about the outside world and caution, and between the siren call of the larger world and fear of the other. It may appear in memories that involve parental restrictions (no playing in the street, riding one's bike beyond the backyard or going to a friend's house).

Places like gardens and patios are safe, intermediate spaces between the home and the outside world. They are like a foyer, neither entirely inside nor completely outside. While accidents and incidents cannot be prevented, the child is relatively safe there. In that respect, the garden is a limited-risk training ground where she can experiment and practice exploring the world. It feeds the imagination while providing a protected space.[5] Of course the garden boundary may be violated, literally or symbolically. I remember two young gypsies who sold pins and knick-knacks door to door. When they saw me staring at them from behind the gate, they called out to me. Their ragged clothing and long hair made a strong impression on me (the Beatles had not yet arrived on the scene). I remember, soon afterwards, an adult warning me to stay away from gypsies because they were known to kidnap children. That wasn't true, of course, but I remember being terrified. From that day on, I kept my distance from the gate.

DENNIS IS GOING AROUND IN CIRCLES, WHILE DAVID CAN'T MANAGE TO GET UP AND GO (THE CONNECTION BETWEEN EXPERIENCE AND MEMORY)

A young man—let's call him Dennis—came to see me after breaking up with a young woman he'd met three months earlier. He had been very happy and entertained great hopes for the future of the relationship. One day, she told him that she loved to travel and was planning a ten-day trip to the United States. He couldn't leave his job for that long, so he tried to dissuade her from going. She didn't understand. Why should she cancel the trip just because he couldn't go with her? That evening, things got nasty and tempers flared. They exchanged harsh words, accusations and criticism. The young woman grew tired of arguing and tried to soothe him one last time but ultimately withdrew in silence.

The next morning, Dennis went to see her to apologize for his unjustified behavior. A week later, they were having dinner with friends. The conversation returned to the same topic and the conflict raged again. Exasperated, shocked and humiliated by being abused in front of her friends, the young woman told Dennis she wanted to end the relationship. His first reaction was that she was just trying to scare him. He didn't respond and went to work. However, a few hours later, they had a phone conversation and she repeated that she had made up her mind. Dennis was devastated and made an appointment to see me a few days later.

As soon as he began talking, two words came to mind as I listened to the way he spoke and observed his effort to control the conversation: demanding and resistant. From all appearances, this person was used to being in charge. I decided to look for evidence of this behavior in his past to see whether that might shed any light. Point-blank, I asked him for a childhood memory. "A childhood memory?" he said. "Any memory?" After a short hesitation, he continued, "My friends and I were riding our bikes. We had a large patio. We were riding in circles, going around and around." Unconsciously, of course, Dennis immediately sought the memory that corresponded most closely to his current situation— blocked movement. You can make a game of riding in circles, but when you get on a bike, you usually have a destination in mind. The important point is that in this memory, the object associated with movement (the bicycle) was diverted from its common use. Reinterpreted in the context of this relationship, this means, "Since I can't use my wings to fly, you can't, either. You must remain in your assigned place and, like me, develop within limits." Psychoanalysis would probably reveal that Dennis comes from a restrictive family environment.

This insight is particularly interesting because without the memory-based approach, I probably would have assumed that this was a classic case of jealousy and would have missed the real issue.

In a later session, Dennis began by discussing his doubts about this method. "What bothers me is that you can draw so many conclusions from a single memory," he said. "Sure, I chose that one, but what if I had chosen a different one? What if I had found one related to my love life, since that's my problem?" I made two comments in response. First, I pointed out that this really was a textbook case and that I'm not always lucky enough to be happen upon such transparent memories. Second, I noted that it was not by accident that he had sought out that particular memory. When someone reads us a little too clearly, it's irritating. "Yes," Dennis acknowledged, "'If, if, if.'"

He went on to say, "This issue raises an ambiguity that I have always sensed in myself. On the one hand, I am someone who wants to grow, but on other hand, I feel that I'm restricted. My life would certainly be easier if I could move forward instead of . . ." We finished the sentence together, both saying, "Going around in circles?" Voilà! He continued the thought. "Those restrictions come from my upbringing. My father always played an important role in my choices. He would question and challenge every single one. I know that those restrictions led me to make choices that don't really reflect who I am."

David had been in a turbulent relationship with a young woman for three years. They had separated and reconciled several times. "I don't understand," he told me. "I can't leave." I asked him for a childhood memory. His face showed surprise. After a moment, he said, "I was slapped when I was learning to tie my shoelaces. I kept doing it all wrong, and my father slapped me. The second time, I did it correctly." He added, "I talked to my father about that recently and told him how much that had upset me. He said, 'It worked, didn't it?'"[6]

To understand the dynamic of this memory and its relationship to blocked movement, we need to focus on the shoes, not the slap (although there's plenty to say on that score). Here they symbolize movement, and the difficulty tying them should be understood as blocking movement, or at least making it difficult. We can interpret the statement, "I can't tie my shoes properly," symbolically as, "It's hard for me to leave." (Would you get very far if your shoelaces were untied?) If I were to take a more psychoanalytic perspective, I would probably even draw a connection between David's shoelaces (*lacets* in French) and Dennis's roundabout bicycle course (also *lacets!*). I might do the same by playing with the words David used when discussing his relationship. In English, you talk about getting together, breaking up and getting back together, but in French, we say tying, untying and retying.

THE GOAL OF THE VOYAGE IS TO RETURN

English has several words for the French word *voyage*—trip, journey, travel and, yes, voyage, which is often used, for example, in the context of an "ocean voyage." Think of Marco Polo's journey to China. The goal was to explore the world but also to return to home port, with treasures filling the boat's hold (if possible).

Curiously, the word "voyage" is also used in certain rites of passage. The participant must embark on a journey, during which he will be tested. At the end of this turbulent voyage, he will be recognized and accepted as a member of the brotherhood or tribe. The rite of passage thus involves sending the individual away, actually or symbolically, from the bosom of the community, launching him on a voyage where his life will be put in danger and then bringing him back. When he returns, he will be purified and, in a sense, transformed. In any event, he will be different.

The purpose of the voyage is not to leave but to return as a changed person.[7] Something inside the person must die for something else to be born. A voyage always involves exploring the larger world. The person sets off alone and returns to recount to the others what he has discovered or experienced.

Our movement-related memories symbolize this dimension of exploration. It involves both setting out on a quest to learn about the external world and returning to nourish our internal world. These memories always include this rite of passage element, which is why I think we must take it into account in our analysis.

Let's take stock here. In addition to the standard methods for interpreting memories that are accessible to anyone—including common sense—you now have two tools with which to evaluate, through your memories, the counterbalancing forces of your personality. The elements of the principle of core nuclear relationships (mother, father, siblings, and others; appearing in order, out of order or not at all) provide information on your relationships with others. The presence or absence of outwardly directed movement and its nature (present, symbolic or blocked) will help you understand your relationship to the external world and your internal world. These two tools are inextricably linked. In addition, they do not preclude the use of the more conventional approaches to analyzing memories, as I have described them. By using these tools and elements simultaneously, you can sketch out a reasonably faithful portrait of your personality and, probably, your character.

In the next chapter, I will conduct a hands-on exercise and interpret the three memories I recounted early in the book. Given the constraints, I cannot provide an exhaustive interpretation, but I will cover the major points. I will also offer two other examples of memories. One raises the issue of self-assertion and the other, self-effacement.

CHAPTER 8

Interpreting
Childhood Memories:
A Series of Examples

Time it was, and what a time it was, it was
A time of innocence, a time of confidences.
—Simon and Garfunkel, "Bookends"

From Catching Butterflies To Passing on Values

When I asked you to write down your memories, I suggested that you highlight or underline the core memories to distinguish them from the details added later. That's what I'm going to do here. The memories appear in italics, and the additional details are in regular typeface.

That order is important because the first words that come to mind are a direct expression of our unconscious, while the details we add may result from a quick thought or a desire to direct things in a certain way. I have learned to give each word the importance it deserves and understand that it's not by accident that a particular piece of information or specific word precedes another. Of course, there are no "word police" on duty here to challenge how you choose to express yourself.[1] The issue is to determine the priority our unconscious assigns to our words, just as we may "listen" to slips of the tongue or (subconsciously) deliberate mistakes.

Here is my first memory: *I am in a garden that feels a bit neglected. I am holding a brightly colored butterfly net, trying to catch the butterflies flitting through the tall grass.* There is a henhouse at the far end of the garden. This memory is set at my aunt and uncle's house in the Vendée region of France. It is a sunny day and I'm wearing shorts. I must be around six.

As you observe, this first memory involves movement (the Vendée), although it is a secondary element, not a primary one. I specified the location only in my comments, when I noted that my family used to go there in the summer when I was little.

The garden is the most important element. Earlier, we saw the garden as a transitional space between the interior of the house, which is a safe place, and the outside world. This garden is not at my house, but at my aunt and uncle's, so it conveys a stronger sense of the unknown. The garden is an enclosed space. Unlike other people–claustrophobics, for example—I am not bothered by confined spaces and even find them pleasant. When I was a child, I spent several years in boarding school. As a young man, I lived in West Berlin for nine years before the Wall fell, and I now live in a small housing development.

I said the garden was neglected. Neglect expresses disorder, so the garden is like a miniature jungle. As a child, I felt I was being thrown into a strange world where everything was difficult and nothing came easily. Perhaps being left-handed heightened that sense. In the 1950s, left-handed people were made to feel different from everyone else, and learning to write was no small matter for me. (Perhaps that's why, as an adult, I took up writing.) I have always felt a need to create order out of disorder. Even today, as an adult, I still feel that's my job. That's what I do with my therapy patients, who no longer have a clear vision of what is happening in their life. I also tend to my own garden, so to speak, by reading, studying and reflecting on myself, others and the world. As you might imagine, that kind of landscaping project is never finished. With its tall grass, this garden seems to correspond to my daily environment.

Now let's take a look at the butterfly net in my hand. We're not talking about big game hunting here. The central message that this element conveys is found elsewhere and should be interpreted as a desire to catch or, in symbolic terms, to grasp. This corresponds to my personality too. I love trying to catch, grasp and understand subtle and hidden meanings, which is ideal for someone in my profession. Isn't the psychologist's role to catch the phrase, the unsaid, the slip of the tongue, the behavior or the resistance in "mid-flight" and turn it back to the person in a different form? I also absorb everything I can. I am hungry for everything that might be of interest or value. I have an epicurean side that wants to enjoy every possible experience and take advantage of every opportunity. In a way, the butterfly net symbolizes all that—catching the fleeting and the delicate, which not everyone can perceive.

You probably noticed that this first memory refers only to me. No one else is present. Only my aunt and uncle are mentioned here, and just as geographic reference points. I am alone. Indeed, I don't mind solitude. I enjoy it, as long as it's short-term. That said, I do need company (the need for social interaction appears in the second memory, where my siblings and games play a role). However, I prefer individual sports (skiing, squash, tennis and swimming). I don't enjoy team sports and I'm not particularly drawn to nature. Unless I'm with friends and the outing involves a particular activity like completing a fitness trail or mushroom hunting, I'm perfectly happy to stay home. In truth, I am a city dweller. I love Paris, the smell of the metro, the cars and the bars that open out onto the sidewalk.

I don't mind going places (like the Vendée), but I prefer safe destinations (like gardens). I'm not an adventure traveler. I like to feel secure while I'm exploring the world. I enjoy discoveries, physical activity, social interaction and movement, but boundaries and protected spaces suit me very well. I am always happy to find a new destination or restaurant but tend to be loyal to my regular haunts. "Freedom within limits freely agreed to," James Joyce would say. The henhouse at the other end of the yard thus corroborates what I've just noted. While it conveys the sense of nourishment (also present in my third memory, which includes an indoor market), I see it as synonymous to the garden. A henhouse is a semienclosed space where birds can circulate between the interior and the exterior. Rather than fly, they flutter.

This first memory says a lot about my personality and tastes. Now let's see what the second one tells us.

Second memory: *My sister Annick falls down the stairs while riding on my brother Yves's back, breaking one of her upper teeth.* This occurred in the house where we lived when I was little. The staircase was pretty steep. I don't remember this myself, but I was told that the accident happened because I tickled them and they lost their balance. I must have been four or five.

This second memory features siblings at their most sociable—at play. We were playing in the house (a safe space) but unfortunately, things took a wrong turn and the game ended in an accident. This safe space may not have been as safe as it appeared, however. When I was very young (just over a year old), a baby-sitter struck me repeatedly over several days. I have no memory of the incident. My mother realized what was going on when she saw the marks on my body. My brothers and sister, who had been silenced with threats of reprisal if they said anything, spoke up, and the woman was fired immediately. For me, the home—a safe space (the mother's belly, I often say)—was also a dangerous place. Although I don't remember the incident, I think I exploited it and took advantage of my "victim" status, which I managed to use, and abuse, throughout my childhood. One of my mother's regular refrains was, "Stop picking on your little brother," when I was the one who had provoked my siblings.

This second memory raises the issue of responsibility and guilt. Curiously, I don't remember my involvement. I remember that we were laughing and having fun. I don't ever remember being guilty of the charges made against me soon after the accident. It's natural to look for a scapegoat when something unfortunate happens, but it's also natural to forget what we don't want to know. Regardless, my emotional memory certainly bears the mark of family disapproval, although I do not recall my parents chastising or punishing me. At that moment, I left the paradise of childhood innocence.

This event corresponds to the image of the difficult child I became. Guilt and responsibility arose regularly as issues in my life, first, in terms of my own behavior as a fairly negligent child and adolescent. Later, as an adult, I sublimated those behaviors and sought to behave ethically and take responsibility for myself and others.[2]

While I was working on this section of the book, Annick called to say hello and catch up. I used the opportunity to ask if she had the same memory of that incident. No, she answered. She didn't remember that I tickled them, but that I had tripped my brother (which is worse, in my opinion). She wasn't riding on his back, but on his shoulders. She was surprised that I still felt guilty because she didn't think that the accident was very serious. In truth, I think that although she is minimizing the event (because she always adored me), the loss of that tooth, which she kept until she was sixteen, must have made her feel very self-conscious. This episode reveals, once again, how two people can experience the same situation differently. This brings me to my third memory.

Third memory: *I am with my mother at the market. She is next to me and suddenly bursts into tears.* We were in a covered market in Nice, on the French Riviera. It was just the two of us. I was very young, perhaps five, and I was upset. "Don't cry, Mommy," I said.

This memory deals primarily with nourishment, both physical and emotional, represented by the market (nourishment) and the mother (the maternal breast), and refers to the mother-child dyad. I'm surprised that my unconscious would seek out an episode like this one. As the fourth and last child in the family, I rarely spent time alone with my mother during the first seven years of my life. At first glance, this memory might seem sad because my mother cries, but I'm not sure about that. Rather, I see it as the expression of a desire for a symbiotic relationship with her. I also appear here as the person who comforts my mother. During adolescence, I often played that role with others, which raises the two fundamental qualities that a psychotherapist needs: the ability to empathize and to identify with others.

As a child, I was never the leader in my relationships with others. From adolescence, I preferred two-person relationships. Because I was good at listening and discussing problems, people often treated me as a confidant. Although I find groups, seminars and trainings very satisfying, my primary activity today is still individual consultation—the work that two people do. I really enjoy one-on-one conversations. I also love reading, which I consider a special conversation between the author and me, and you've seen that I often refer to my conversation with you.

Now let's examine the relationship among these memories.

First, the garden, house and covered market are all enclosed spaces. Together, they create a feeling of protection. My memories and style of life are consistent, as I am probably a man who needs to feel secure in a recognizable space.

You may have noticed that the classic core nuclear relationships do not appear in my three memories. My father is absent, so you won't be surprised to learn that my parents divorced very early. I was six when they separated. As far as I recall, my father was not very present during my early childhood. Although he never struck me, I was very frightened of him, especially when he frowned (which he did often). Although he was not present to introduce me to the larger world (as you remember, I said that that is the father's role), I almost never had to deal with the paternal superego, which can be harmful, especially to boys. As French philosopher Jean-Paul Sartre said, "When fathers have projects, children have destinies."

The second memory seems to be the least significant of the three. While a sibling-related memory could have provided information on my difficult relationships with my brother and sisters (given my status as the youngest), this one doesn't. In fact, I think its only purpose is to underscore the insecurity that can exist within the home. If the baby-sitter had abused me when I was older, at around two or three years of age, that memory could have emerged as one of those "headline events," but it didn't happen that way.

My successive careers all involve that place where the external and internal worlds intersect and seem to correspond to the three memories I recounted. I've taught French at Berlitz language schools and worked as a translator, interpreter, psychotherapist and writer. Each career involves transmitting or passing on, whether by teaching a class, translating words from one language to another, interpreting memories, dreams and behavior or presenting my research findings to readers. Incidentally, this also corresponds to my self-image, as I've always thought of myself as a transmitter of values.

You can see how closely the memories recounted relate to the individual's current situation. Still, some issues were too personal for me to include in a book. Freud referred to that dilemma when he published *The Interpretation of Dreams*. In the foreword to the first edition, he wrote, "I could not resist the temptation to mitigate my indiscretions by omissions and substitutions; but wherever I have done so the value of the example cited has been very definitely diminished."[3] Of course, the three memories I decoded for you cannot compare to Freud's deep personal involvement throughout the five hundred-odd pages of his book, but the problem is the same.

GERALD DOESN'T WANT TO OWE ANYONE ANYTHING

I sometimes offer company-based continuing education courses, which is how I had the pleasure of meeting a young man—let's call him Gerald—who was having interpersonal problems at work. He had already been referred to me several times. Despite the unstated suggestion that it would be a good idea for him to talk to a neutral third party, he had never followed up because he didn't think he had anything to discuss with a therapist. We met first in a hallway and then sat down for a cup of coffee.

Gerald was one of the company's first employees. He had always performed extremely well and had a promising career ahead of him. However, he was quite strong-willed and even rude to his employers, which put him at odds with them. He came close to being fired several times, but the situation had always calmed down. He found it strange that people thought so poorly of him yet sought him out when they needed his help. He had been offered a position with greater responsibility during a company reorganization.

He liked challenges and relished taking a project from start to finish. But once the bulk of the work was completed, he got bored. People at work called him "the mercenary." That didn't bother him. He described himself as frank, honest and sincere, unwilling to tolerate petty lies or cruel behavior.

The company offered him training to upgrade his skills, but he changed his mind after accepting. "School has never been my thing, even if I always did get good grades," he said. "I never really liked it. I don't like the educational system and I can't stand the mediocrity of the instructors. If a teacher is wrong, I'll fight like crazy to prove it. You can imagine how far that gets me."

Acceleration seemed to be a theme in his life. He was precocious in a range of areas, from sports (sail boarding) to women.

By the time he was twenty, he already had a child. "I was always out of step compared to others my age," he said. "When I was sixteen, my friends were twenty-five or older."

A sense of resistance or going against the tide seemed to emerge from Gerald's comments. It was as if he refused to submit to anything or anyone. I could have easily identified this as a hysterical tendency (I'm thinking of the line in the aria from *Carmen*, "If you don't love me, I love you"), but it didn't seem quite that clear. I was particularly preoccupied by the notion of his being "out of step." I thought a childhood memory might shed some light, so I asked him, point-blank, "How about if we try out a little psychology? What do you think? Can you tell me a very early memory—from your very early childhood, if possible?" Almost immediately, he said, "When I was three years old, I got lost. We were walking down the main street in my town. I think it was a pedestrian zone. I was with my mother and my grandmother. I saw a baby in a stroller and when I looked up again, I didn't see either of them. They looked for me everywhere and even called the fire department and the police. In the meantime, I went back alone to my grandparents' house, a few blocks away. I walked down the sidewalk, crossed two streets and made it back."

"So you managed all alone?" I said. "Yes, I did," he answered. Then I asked him what he thought his memory revealed. "That I managed just fine on my own?" I both nodded and shook my head. "I think that in addition to, 'I can manage all alone,' your memory is saying, 'I don't need anyone,' and even, 'I don't want to owe anyone anything.'"

He was starting to get interested in what I had to say. "I never thought about it like that, but it's true," he said. "For example, I have no interest in buying on credit. If I'm going to buy a car, I pay cash. I can't stand the idea of being in debt. I do things for other people when I can, but, personally, I never borrow anything that belongs to someone else."

"So when you said earlier, somewhat bitterly, I thought, that you're treated very poorly but that people come to you when they need you, your bitterness might not have been appropriate," I went on. "Maybe you are responsible. Since you don't want to be in anyone's debt, they have to seek you out, as if to say, 'We need you.' Maybe that's also why you don't do very well in management. A boss necessarily has to 'ask' his or her employees to do things. You feel better when other people come to you. That could also explain, at least in part, why you resisted coming to talk to me. Perhaps you didn't want to owe me anything."

This memory highlighted a kind of behavior that neither Gerald nor the company directors could have suspected. What might appear simply as a bad temper could be reinterpreted as having roots deep in his childhood. There is a considerable difference between "I can manage" and "I don't want to owe anyone anything." The message that was probably imprinted deep in Gerald's brain was, "You thought little children are dependent on adults? Well, I showed you that I can do just fine without you." Gerald could now understand the real motivations that his attitude obscured and will probably be in a position to make decisions that reflect his own best interest.

Valerie Withdraws into the Background

Don't assume that analyzing memories is always productive. Despite the hundreds upon hundreds of memories I have listened to, and despite my experience in interpreting them, to my surprise, sometimes a memory tells me nothing. And I mean nothing! I try to understand the connections, but I can't find any. A situation like that can challenge my entire theory. You need a real shot of optimism to keep from simply closing up shop and refusing to do this anymore.

A memory that reveals nothing may express a way of life or a life problem that the person is unconsciously trying to erase. Some people go through life wearing masks, as child psychiatrist Bruno Bettelheim said, and others are discreet and reserved. They are not hiding in life's shadows, but are sensitive, simple people.

One day, Valerie, an energetic fifty-year-old woman, said to me, "If I'm not happy, it's because I refuse to let myself be. We live in an unjust society. I am perfectly happy not to earn a lot of money. I would be ashamed to have too much, compared to those who have nothing." I absorbed her words but at the same time, although I don't know why, I came to feel that she was complaining about her situation. To learn more about this attitude, which seemed to do her a disservice (in general, everyone wants to earn a good living), I asked her to tell me the first early childhood memory that popped into her head. "It would have to be in the country, where I spent my early childhood," she began. "The house where I lived. My mother took care of my brothers herself, but I was raised by a young nanny who was barely eighteen.

I don't know why my parents hired her, because we already had people working in the house and my mother wasn't working. What's odd is that my only photos show the nanny holding me. There are none with my mother. I remember when that nanny left. I was very sad."

You will notice that there are very few pieces of information here. The only detail that caught my attention was her characterization of the setting, when she emphasized, "The house where I lived." As you know, from a psychoanalytic perspective, the house is often understood to mean the mother's womb. I decided to put this detail aside for the moment and was about to ask her for a second memory, when she cut me off, saying, "What I just told you reminds me of something I'd completely forgotten. When I was a little girl, I was always afraid that I wasn't really my parents' child. I was afraid that the hospital had made a mistake."

This memory, which came back to her "by accident" at just the right moment, led me to conclude that I was on the right track. That is, if I am not my parents' child, I am not part of the family line, I don't exist legally and my life is based on a mistake. I am tolerated but don't have a real place within the family. Therefore, I should stay in the background and make myself small. Furthermore, if I am not part of the family, I will feel guilty about belonging or, in other words, about owning. If that's how you felt about yourself, it would be difficult to set off like an Alexander the Great to conquer life and the world and embrace the quest for fame, fortune and renown.

This dynamic of "I am, I'm not" had reduced her stature as a person. She felt that she had to withdraw into the background, so she became a withdrawn woman. And her memory expressed that way of life—hidden and secret.

There is nothing wrong with living in secrecy. It's a question of temperament. Some people need to shine, while others need to not be visible. Those people find it difficult to take advantage of a stroke of luck or the good things life has to offer. They feel they are not entitled to such good fortune. They pull back rather than engage in human exchange. At the same time, they are often very interesting, cultured individuals because they have a rich interior life, are very curious and love to read. They don't lack interest, but feel that they are uninteresting. The complex created by the discrepancy between their self-image and reality leads them to flee interpersonal relationships and avoid people. Choosing to withdraw, they appear to be disinterested in others when other people affect them deeply.

From a general initial comment about society and its faults, Valerie managed to recall and verbalize a memory of a very old, deep fear (not being her parents' child). This fear points to the path she may have followed to pursue a style of life corresponding to a profound experience. A childhood memory that initially appeared not to mean anything, in the primary sense of the term, turned out to be meaningful when interpreted in relation to what was said and to the person's style of life: I withdraw, therefore I am.

Every interpretation is based on the assumption that reliable information and a stable foundation support the analysis. However, like dreams, memories are eminently subjective creations. How, then, can we distinguish between reality and fiction? First, we can begin by characterizing the situation. In some cases, the "truth" is insignificant and I'd even go so far as to say that it is unimportant altogether. For example, were you in Seattle or Chicago when you lost the plastic watch that your godfather gave you for your sixth birthday? In other circumstances, the truth is critical, particularly when harassment, physical or psychological violence or sexual abuse are involved, because the individual has had to struggle with vagueness, uncertainty and denial for years, blocking the work of acknowledgment, mourning and healing.

Wounds of the spirit heal if we treat them. To do that, we must address them openly. That is not always easy because in the midst of the storm, we can lose our bearings quickly and come to doubt everything, even our own memories.

Part Four

Wounds

CHAPTER 9

True or
False Memories?

The memory of those first five years of my life
begins to come back, the years that my grandmother
Paulina and everyone else cloaked in
a mantle of mystery.
—ISABEL ALLENDE, *PORTRAIT IN SEPIA*

DON'T WORRY, I WON'T TAKE YOU AT YOUR WORD

When people begin psychotherapy, they are often uncomfortable about sharing their memories because they have difficulty distinguishing between what they actually experienced and what they remember. Out of concern for authenticity, they want to warn the therapist about the accuracy of a particular piece of information. When necessary, I try to reassure patients that their feelings are completely normal. The events and anecdotes they recount are necessarily filtered through their own subjectivity and cannot, therefore, be considered objectively "true." I often say jokingly, "Don't worry, I won't take you at your word." People usually smile at this paradoxical comment but are reassured that I have heard their message.

When we're dealing with memories, the "truth" is unimportant. How we present those memories is much more interesting. The first memory from my childhood included a butterfly net. As I thought more about it, I realized that it was a fishing net that my mother bought me in a store that sold surf fishing supplies. The interesting point here is how my adult memory transformed the use of that object. Why didn't I remember going shrimp fishing? Or putting the net on my brother's head like a hat? Or putting it on my face like a fencing mask? Those experiences didn't come back to me until later. That is where we find the meaning of the memory, as well as its mystery and latent meaning. Through the memory work, my unconscious reorganized the information it needed so that the recollection would correspond to my style of life.

The unconscious does not need "the truth." The only truth that matters for the unconscious is the feeling created by the experience and how it can arrange that feeling to fit into our larger psychic economy. Our weaknesses and resistances are also filtered through our subjectivity and may alter our vision of our memories. The unconscious will generally revise the history of the difficult times in our life—the unpleasant, painful times, when we suffer and experience unhappiness, when failure, humiliation and disgrace can damage our image—and will place the seal of its truth on the new version.

Everyone close to us who has marked our childhood or played a role in our early life has his or her own perception of events too. When those projections conflict with ours, things get complicated. Sometimes these differences in perception operate on a relatively anecdotal level, as in the incident of my sister's broken tooth. However, at other times, the stakes are much higher.

THE MEMORIES THAT OTHERS DENY US

While most experts agree that the earliest childhood memories date from around three or four years of age, some memories date from a much younger age. This can be disconcerting for parents, who simply do not believe that a child can have such early memories. Rather than accepting the child's account or even praising her for her memory, they immediately try to prove that such and such an event could not have occurred and that the child is mistaken or telling stories. Of course, some details of the recalled past are insignificant. However, when more important issues are at stake, a parent's doubt, mockery or vindictiveness can confuse the child, who must then abandon some part of her childhood to avoid conflict with the parent. In the previous chapter, I told you that I was abused by a baby-sitter when I was around one. I have no memory of this incident, but someone else—you, might have been able to recall it, even from that age. This isn't just a matter of principle or a case in which a child refuses to give in, against all evidence and simply out of stubbornness. In psychotherapy, I tend to give considerable credence to children's memories because I see no reason for them to lie. In addition, the details they recount usually leave no room for doubt. It seems to me that parents are not pleased when their offspring show early signs of exceptional ability, as if that somehow diminished the adults. However, children must be allowed their own legacy of memories because even if their recollections include errors, they are part of a broader experience that is fundamental to the child, precisely because she has verbalized it.

Other parents take a sly pleasure in hiding the family's past out of shame, a desire for secrecy or, perhaps absurdly, because they want to maintain their superiority or power over the child. After all, it's easy to dismiss a younger person's memory when you have the advantage of age. If the older person refuses to give in, there is no point in arguing, no matter how solid the arguments. I remember a session with a young woman, Danielle, who had a childhood memory of hearing her grandmother talk about her Jewish roots. Later, Danielle's mother always made it a point of honor to deny that possibility, claiming that the grandmother could never have said such a thing and that she was Italian, pure and simple. *Basta!*

We can sense the dilemma in this conflict. Who should Danielle believe? Can a person make such a basic mistake? Why would her grandmother lie? Why would her mother insist on denying that reality? Danielle felt robbed of part of her identity. As she became more insistent, her mother took an even more inflexible, authoritarian position. Danielle refused to concede and questioned the rest of the family, including her great-grandmother. The older woman, after insisting that she knew nothing, finally acknowledged that her family was indeed Jewish on her mother's side and had lived in Armenia before emigrating to Italy. This story about family roots might not seem particularly important, but Danielle had met a young man from an observant Jewish family that would never have permitted a mixed marriage.

As far as I know, the story had a happy ending. But how many other people are stranded, faced with doubt or denial, because a family refuses to acknowledge certain events or facts? Many of us have been robbed of part of our past, whether the loss involves family origins, the hidden presence of a lover or mistress in the mother's or father's life or a period of poverty that the parents want to minimize or even avoid discussing.

It can be very painful when close family members deny a memory. The individual affected may find that she is challenging her own memory and mental faculties and, in the end, herself. This form of denial can also lead to serious physical and emotional problems if it prevents the individual from gaining access to her full history. The situation is even more difficult when circumstances such as genocide require the individual to work through grief, but the event itself is denied.

Memories denied to us can thus become memories we deny ourselves, as if we use the harm someone does to us to hurt ourselves. This can produce an insidious, latent wound and sometimes a very visible one. Both cases suggest that we are dealing with genuine trauma.

This brings us to the issue of family secrets and what is left unsaid. Psychotherapist Anne Ancelin-Schützenberger's work addresses these questions.[1] She paints a gripping and moving picture of the burden that family secrets impose when the individual's psyche perceives them but they are not acknowledged at a conscious level. She points to cases of serious illnesses, like cancer, that have unexpectedly gone into remission when family secrets hidden for several generations are acknowledged. "I work with what I call the genosociogram . . . by constructing the past, often over two centuries (seven to nine generations), and sometimes over a longer period."[2] She analyzes events "'that people are ashamed of,' or a 'painful situation' for the family, things people 'disapprove of,' that are 'unpleasant,' 'suspicious' and 'bad'. . . It could be a murder, a suspicious death, tuberculosis, syphilis, commitment to an institution, a stay in a psychiatric hospital, imprisonment, a bankruptcy, a 'shameful' illness, adultery or incest. This involves forgetting someone who was disgraced or disgraced the family, something that people were ashamed of and did not talk about."[3]

We find this kind of tragedy, resulting from what is left unsaid, in the memories that families deny the child (something that is not discussed will be forgotten). Although the etiology may be different, the impact on the child's emotional equilibrium and health will be similar. I will address the acute aspects of this problem when I discuss the silence surrounding sexual abuse and incest.

MEMORIES THAT DO NOT BELONG TO US (SECONDHAND MEMORIES)

We carry memories that do not belong to us. I call them secondhand memories. They are common enough to deserve attention and are particularly interesting when they appear first in a series of three memories.

Recently a friend (I'll call him John) asked me about the subject of my next book. When I told him that it would address the living structure of memories, he said, "I have *absolutely* no interest in memories." I found his reaction fascinating, so I asked him to tell me one of his, despite his lack of interest.

"A real memory or one that somebody told me?" he asked.

"Whichever you like," I answered.

"I have one that was told to me. I was a year old. My mother was hospitalized and I was placed in foster care. The whole thing is still somewhat mysterious."

Secondhand memories are unusual. If we include them in our biography, there must be a reason for doing so. I analyze them as part of our personal mythology. What is a myth? In simple terms, I define it as the story of an individual or well-known person that has entered the public domain. Our personal mythologies distinguish our life story from others and usually involve something extraordinary. If an adult has told, retold and commented on the incident, it must really be remarkable. To return to my second childhood memory, you will recall that I told you I had adopted the story about being struck by a baby-sitter and had benefited from the status of victim during my childhood.

The uniqueness of myths may also result from a fault or a discriminatory experience. For example (I'm making some of this up), everybody knows that Martha (or Fred or David) moved her bowels in Uncle Robert's car when she was three because she came down with a sudden case of diarrhea. This kind of negative mythology is not always easy to live with, especially when family members recount the story at every opportunity and laugh about it. My older sister used to eat cherries and give the pits to my little sister, who would swallow them as they were handed to her. I don't have a personal memory of that incident, but do I remember that we repeated it often as a funny story. Just as my sister had some difficulty expelling all those pits, the myth followed her for years and was painful to live with too.

We all have secondhand memories that exist alongside our own. From that perspective, childhood and family life are fertile ground in terms of relationships, where individual and collective histories take shape, jostle each other and develop. John may deny an interest in memories, but they do concern him. They speak of him and his unconscious.

FALSE MEMORIES AND MENTAL MANIPULATION

The previous section leads me to refer briefly to an issue that has received considerable attention, particularly in the United States: so-called repressed memories of alleged sexual abuse that some psychotherapists and psychoanalysts say they have uncovered in their patients' childhood. While the problem is well-known, the scientific world still lacks perspective on this issue.[4] How should we think about it?

Even a young psychotherapist will encounter individuals in his or her practice who report incest. Some patients describe the trauma in particularly clear terms. The therapist's job is to accept those pain-filled words and help the individual channel them and gain relief from the burden they represent. At other times, the words are not so transparent and the therapist must untangle the web of thoughts, feelings, emotions and doubts trapping the person's memory. A therapist who lacks experience or, conversely, has become blasé may be tempted to try to rescue the situation or bring things to a close quickly by arbitrarily "guiding" the patient's memories, even going so far as to flout truth and the facts. Imagine how confusing it would be to consult a therapist on an unrelated issue and suddenly be confronted with a horrific "memory" that is supposed to be yours.

I believe that every therapist has occasionally tried to speed the process by being provocative or suggestive, just to elicit a response. That might be understandable in dealing with what we would consider minor issues, but such an action is unacceptable in the context of problems as serious as incest. The vast majority of therapists know the danger of that kind of projection. If information or suspicions emerge from a secret or a doubt voiced during a session or just as the patient gets up to leave, the therapist's ethics will prompt him or her to respond to that information calmly and patiently. In any event, memories must always be allowed to emerge on their own. The therapist must not seek them out for some unknown purpose.

CHAPTER 10

Memories and Trauma

Hopefulness, rather than hope,
is the driving force in my life.

—TIM GUÉNARD, *TAGUEURS D'ESPÉRANCE*

TRAUMA IS ONE of most serious issues raised by memories, particularly childhood traumas. These experiences take different forms, including trauma an individual experienced or to which he or she was subjected. They also include traumatic situations in which the child might have been involved or trauma caused others, whether or not he was responsible.

Whatever their nature, these traumas work through the child's memories and inevitably distort his self-perception. In a logical but cruel sequence, this changed self-perception then alters the child's sense of others, the world and human existence. I will return to that issue when I address the question of guilt.

Some children manage to come out on top even after being subjected to trauma, although we don't know how to explain their success. Meeting a third person—a sympathetic teacher, an understanding youth worker, a kind, concerned neighbor or even a homeless person who becomes a friend—can transform the child's fate. Unfortunately, that does not always happen. The individual may not be available at the right moment or the child may not be able to listen or confide.

Let's not mince words here. The images associated with childhood trauma would fill a catalog of miseries too painful to describe: spite, cruelty, treachery, injustice, arbitrariness, confinement, abuse, mistreatment, sadism, perversion, physical and psychological violence, sexual aggression and incest. Every day, all over the world, millions of children are victims of cruelty, debauchery and barbarism perpetrated by relatives or neurotic, degenerate, vicious and unbalanced adults.[1]

We should not try to establish a "hierarchy of harm" to assess objective degrees of damage. We cannot rank injustice, cowardice, unrepentance, horror and abjection. This is not about revisiting the meaning of evil. We are dealing here with a status—victim of abuse—not a scale. The trauma that adults subject children to must be acknowledged as such. Psychologists and psychotherapists must not distort it under the pretext of easing the transition to the work of mourning. If an individual is to emerge from trauma, it must be recognized for what it is.

WHEN AN INDIVIDUAL IS SUBJECTED TO TRAUMA

The dictionary defines trauma as the range of disorders caused by a wound, shock or violent emotion.

How many babies, youngsters and older children experience the arbitrary behavior of adults who claim to raise them or act as authority figures, but demoralize, wound, torture and abuse them instead? How many children live in a state of perpetual stress and anxiety? Violence is not limited to inflicting blows on a body. It can take forms as benign as they are Machiavellian. Pressure, cruelty, innuendo, arguments, harassment and conflicts over principle can sap a child's morale as silently as a cancer can gradually destroy the healthy cells in a body that appears robust. There is a particularly striking discrepancy between the "happy family" image presented to the outside world and the actual psychological violence and insidious pressure eating away at the children.

When I asked a recently separated woman in her forties, a pharmacist, to make a list of the things she feared about her husband (also a pharmacist), she itemized twenty-five separate issues. She found it particularly difficult to talk about her husband's psychological and sometimes physical cruelty toward their children because she had always felt guilty about her inability to protect them. Later I asked her to cross off the fears that no longer troubled her after their separation. Only two remained: the fear of not being her husband's professional equal and not finding another man she could love and who would love her. Now that she was focusing on these issues, I asked her to list the freedoms she had found or rediscovered since the separation. She came up with thirty-two. The first was "the freedom to choose what to wear in the morning" and the last, "the freedom to speak without being afraid of irritating him." This example illustrates how a particular context—often isolation—can lead an individual to infantilize herself in the relationship. Imagine how the children might be treated. Contradictory messages, threats, screams, blackmail, lies and unfounded criticism delivered daily can cause a child to close off or withdraw to avoid pain. How will he maintain his self-esteem? What memories will he have after those years of fear, anxiety and stress?

WHEN AN INDIVIDUAL EXPERIENCES TRAUMA

Whether an individual experiences trauma or observes it, the effects are similar. A little boy may lose an arm in an explosion or may be present at the scene, terrified, without suffering a direct injury. I remember seeing a fight between two men in a public park when I was around eight years old. As one man kicked the other in the face, the victim lay on the ground, half conscious. He was moaning as he crawled, his face and mouth bloody. He could not have hurt anyone in that condition, but the other man continued kicking him in the face. I have witnessed painful scenes in my life, but this one frightened me so much that it will remain engraved in my memory forever.

Painful or violent scenes witnessed in childhood leave an indelible mark because they affect a child's spirit, the part of her that is fragile because still innocent and untouched. Scenes of destruction, injustice, verbal, psychological and physical abuse and horrifying, shocking and inappropriate comments can leave deep marks in a child's psyche. Do you remember Christine, who described the frequent and violent beatings her mother inflicted on her sister, while sparing Christine? You can imagine the respective trauma the two girls suffered; one beaten, the other forced to witness the nightmarish scenes.

TRAUMA IN WHICH A CHILD
IS INVOLVED OR HAS A ROLE

When we discuss traumatic events, we often refer to situations in which children are the targets of adult abuse, but rarely those in which children are the abusers, even if concepts like fault or responsibility do not apply. Children retain vivid memories of such trauma, which can be a source of great pain when recalled regularly. If no one takes action and if the child does not have access to psychotherapy, he will feel the daily weight of silence, shame, guilt, remorse and sadness.

A man once came to see me, referred by his physician. During their conversation, the doctor observed that his patient had major psychological problems the doctor did not feel he could address. In his letter to me, he wrote, "Dear Patrick, I am referring my patient, E.M., who appears to be experiencing the psychological aftereffects of an early tragic experience. I hope that you will be able to help him. Thank-you." (Notice the typical laconic tone regarding a crisis that could be urgent.) As soon as he sat down, the man told me that he felt he had no right to live because he was responsible for his father's death. As I looked at him questioningly, he explained that when he was five, he had gone into the street in front of his house. When his father saw him, he told his son to stay where he was while he got the boy. Believing his son to be in danger, the man ran out into the street, was hit by a car and died on the spot. The children were not allowed to attend his funeral. They and their mother went to live with grandparents. Over time, life resumed. No one ever suggested he was at fault, and the death was treated as an accident. Everyone avoided talking about it and the tragedy was all but forgotten. However, the child became convinced that he had killed his father and believed that he no longer had a right to be happy. Worse, he began to punish himself for his horrible misdeed. The rest of his childhood was marked by self-renunciation and frustration, resignation and sacrifice. No one ever noticed, assuming that his passivity and lack of drive were personality traits. No one imagined that his behavior might have something to do with a debt he was forcing himself to pay. At twenty-three, he became an accountant to please his grandfather. He did well but had no passion for his work. He might have continued living the pale version of life that was his self-imposed punishment, but a young colleague became interested in him. He rejected her advances for months, but in the end, his actions upset her so deeply that she told him what she thought of his behavior and started crying. Her tears broke through the wall he had built and he found himself crying, for no reason, in the doctor's office.

How many of us, as adults, continue to bear a painful sense of responsibility for some family unhappiness, whether an accident, illness or parental suicide? Or for our parents' marital difficulties, separation or divorce? How many of us still hear that voice saying, "If you hadn't been there, I could have . . ."

"If only you hadn't been born. . . ," "If only I hadn't been saddled with you . . ." In the face of such prosecutorial zeal, how could a child not see herself as the guilty party? How could that memory fail to wound like a knife?

TRAUMA OR ACCIDENT THAT A CHILD MAY HAVE CAUSED ANOTHER PERSON

Some childhood memories involve the child subjecting someone else in the family (child or adult) to trauma. That child's distress leaves him at risk of particularly painful recollections, given that his "guilt" appears glaring. The experience will be even harsher if his parents, brothers or sisters take every opportunity to point an accusing finger at him.

I have never treated a child who traumatized another person. However, I do remember a young man who told me about a strange experience he had when he was about eight. He was riding his bike and stopped at a small bridge a few hundred yards from his home to throw a few stones into the water below. A boy about the same age (probably the child of a family staying at a nearby campground) approached the bridge. Without saying a word, he began throwing stones into the water too. All of a sudden, a second boy came up to the first and pushed him against the railing, shoving him so hard that he fell into the water. Luckily the water was relatively deep at that spot, so the fall was not as dangerous as it might have been. Swept away by a light current, the child struggled and started screaming. His father rushed to the scene and pulled him out of the water. In the meantime, the other boy disappeared. This young man couldn't tell me what happened next. He didn't think that his father tried to find the other boy's parents or follow up on the incident. The story ended there. What was going on in the other boy's head? Was he mentally impaired? Why did he push his fellow human being? Did he understand the danger? We'll never know. Nevertheless, we can try to imagine what the consequences might have been if the victim had hit the water on his back or neck and been paralyzed or killed. How would the other child have dealt with that outcome? What would his life have been like? What aftereffects would he have experienced?

Any childish foolishness and any ill-considered action can turn into tragedy. We've all come close, or brought another child close, to catastrophe by carrying our games or quarrels too far. All it takes is for one child to say to another, "I dare you . . ." The second one doesn't want to be called "chicken," so he takes a stupid, pointless risk. Another child shows off to his friend by taking out the gun his father has hidden away. He fires a shot, striking his friend in the chest. There are innumerable examples of children whose games flirt with tragedy. Occasionally their luck runs out and an entire family mourns, immobilized by sorrow.

But what about the other child—the culprit, the aggressor, the guilty party? Who worries about him and his psychological state, his stress, his trauma? Ours may be a caring society, but we're not ready for that. Leniency has its limits. He's guilty? Let him manage on his own. He should be happy to have gotten off so lightly. That's society's unspoken message. If the child has loving and attentive parents and a good teacher, they will keep close watch and help put into words what happened. A close family and school community will be important. But how many families react like that? Experience shows that in the vast majority of cases, guilty children are left on their own. They receive social, medical, educational and psychological services only when (or if) their deviant behavior or criminal actions create problems for the community.

This is a real problem that cannot be addressed simply as a matter of guilt. "Guilty" children are also in psychological danger.

MEMORY, SEXUAL ABUSE AND INCEST

I have many books in my office. They are my tools and my mentors, reminding me not to adopt a narrow analysis or the psychoanalytic orthodoxy of St. Freud, St. Adler, St. Dolto or St. Jung. "No single doctrine renders others unnecessary," as Josef Rattner, my psychotherapist and director of the Berlin Institute for Analytic Psychology, used to say.

I've kept one of those books in plain sight for years—*Toxic Parents,* by Susan Forward.[2] It is a symbol uniting people who have been subjected to family trauma. New patients are almost relieved to see it, as if its presence reassures them that I understand what happened to them. "You've read this book; you understand," they seem to say. "You know this exists. You know I have suffered physical, emotional, psychological or sexual violence and have had painful experiences. I don't need to go on at length or preface what I have to say. You understand."

Susan Forward strongly endorses psychotherapy as a way to resolve recurrent psychological problems related to childhood trauma. At the end of the book, the chapter dealing with incest, "Healing the Incest Wound," begins, "Professional help is a *must* for adults who were sexually abused as children. Nothing in my experience responds more dramatically and completely to therapy, despite the depth of damage."

Indeed, while an individual may be able to sustain a more or less normal life over long periods by repressing the past, painful memories can resurface at unexpected moments, particularly in the case of incest.

Laurel, a forty-year-old woman whose father sexually abused her for years when she was a child, told me, "You can't live your whole life with what your father did to you. I have to move beyond this story because it's over." Laurel is right. It's over. But the emotional memory is still there. It can reemerge without warning, pulling her backward.

Susan Forward offers a particularly effective technique to gain understanding and take action that I use often in dealing with both childhood and more recent trauma. The technique involves writing a letter to the aggressor. By writing down the painful acts that he accuses the assailant of committing, the victim creates a physical distance between the person and the experience. The action gives the emotional trauma a concrete existence and a physical form and content, helping to ease the transition to the work of mourning. Do you remember what Theresa said (Chapter 3)? "I understood that I had to sacrifice the

pain, separate myself from it, give it to the other person—
the psychologist sitting across from me—and finally leave it there
in his office, once and for all." There are other ways to do this, of
course, but the physical act of leaving the letter in the therapist's
office is a powerful symbolic act of separation.

Susan Forward recommends that the letter include four parts:

- This is what you did to me.
- This is how I felt then.
- This is the effect it's had on my life.
- This is what I expect from you now.

After the patient writes the letter, I ask him what he would
like to do with it. If he wants to share it with me, I read it
(silently). If he wants to take it with him, that's fine. If he wants
to dispose of it symbolically (by flushing it down the toilet, for
example), he can do that too. If he wants to leave the letter with
me, I put it in an envelope that I seal with tape. I write his name
and the date on the envelope, file it in my office and remind him
that it belongs to him and I will return it at any time. This approach provides a sanctuary where painful experiences and other
trauma can be buried and allows the individual to gain some distance from the psychotherapy and the psychotherapist.[3]

THE BRAIN MAKES ADJUSTMENTS TO MANAGE THE INTENSITY OF OUR MEMORIES

A memory that calls up a recollection must be related to an event
or circumstance that was powerful enough to leave an impres-

sion. However, if you examine memories from the distant past, you will notice that over time, the initial intense emotional impression has eased or disappeared. Even the bitterest memories seem to lose their sting. For example, my boarding school memories include the supervisors' arbitrary behavior, the awful food we were forced to eat and the cruelty of certain teachers. But strangely, they have lost the emotional power they had at the time. In any event, that power is much weaker today. You could respond that this numbing effect is specific to me and argue that someone else could have a vivid, precise emotional memory of the situation I minimize here. And you'd be right, because we are dealing with extremely personal and subjective perceptions.

However, we know that human beings deal with long, difficult periods by hiding painful memories and trying to remember positive ones. The brain probably sorts through them and chooses those that will limit our suffering. If we had to remember all the disappointments, miseries, betrayals, suffering, injustices, abandonment and traumas we have endured in emotionally precise, detailed terms, we would probably lose our minds. That's also why the body manifests emotional pain as physical pain, including migraines, sore throats, muscle pain, stomachaches and dysmenorrhea, as a way of sounding a warning, alerting us that a particular pressure, or collection of emotional pressures or pain is building and that we need to pay attention. As child psychiatrist Marcel Rufo explains, "The symptom never appears accidentally. It is always connected to an internal psychic event or an external traumatic event. . . . The psyche appeases its anxiety by creating a symptom, not unlike the delirious person's delirium, which offers protection from a world that, for him, is collapsing."[4] To prevent our world from collapsing, the brain oversees and manages the powerful emotions related to our experiences and the memories that follow from them.

This works most of the time, but not always. Difficult or recurring circumstances can weaken the individual and touch a very sensitive spot in his emotional world, as if attacking his personal protective sphere. If nothing is done to treat that anguish, he will retain the memory of the trauma and the emotional shock that accompanied it and probably still does.

It's like witnessing a raging fire. The images are imprinted on us and the intense emotion that the fear produces is engraved in our psychic apparatus. These are two different emotions or, if you prefer, two different layers of trauma. If the subject of fire arises again, the brain does not seek out specific images of the tragedy we experienced (at least not as a matter of priority), but selects the one that best synthesizes the emotion felt then. We can always overcome a painful blow, but what causes problems later is its persistent representation. As Boris Cyrulnik wrote, "A blow hurts, but it is the representation of the blow that causes trauma."[5]

Verbalizing the events that produced the trauma allows the individual to distance himself from them and mourn, although this grief work cannot always be carried out, or at least not completely. As my patient Frances, a young incest victim, said to me, "At least you can try to shift the pain into the category of past experience." The mark and the scar will remain, but the pain will disappear.

THE UNCONSCIOUS ISN'T
INTERESTED IN THE BIG STORY

Sometimes life brings memories back to the surface in unexpected and disturbing ways. When your best friend tells you she's pregnant (a joyous event that fills you with happiness), that news can set the stage for the recurrence of painful early childhood memories. What pathways did your emotional response follow to cause them to resurface? That is still a mystery. Perhaps science will be able to solve it soon. On the other hand, the unconscious does not necessarily consider what we might think of as "headline events" in our lives—violence, profound suffering, an awful situation—in that way or respond to them as such. Individuals who experience this phenomenon sometimes wonder whether they are unfeeling monsters or maybe have a screw loose. I always reassure those patients that they are normal and even talk about the "healthy" nature of the adjustment the unconscious has made. If their early memories are not uniformly marked by that shock, then the unconscious has done its job, as illustrated by youngsters some psychologists call "unbreakable children."[6] Neuropsychiatrist and writer Boris Cyrulnik's work on resilience is well-known and the notion of resilience has almost become an everyday term. He sees resilience as a natural process. At any given moment, our identity is woven from our physical, emotional and expressive environments. If just one of those gives way, if a single stitch is dropped, the fabric tears. However, if someone offers a single source of aid (for example, help and protection), the weaving can resume and the fabric will mend. However, he notes, "We cannot speak of resilience until much later, when the adult, finally mended, acknowledges the storminess of his childhood."[7]

It may take years for a person to allow early childhood memories of violent trauma to surface spontaneously, not because the individual consciously refuses to let that happen but because the unconscious has either found a way to repress those memories as a form of protection (when we are afraid, the best response is often to forget) or because he has completed his mourning process.

This grief work does not necessarily require a therapist. The right person can enter your life, help make up for the unhealthy past and create an opening for a promising future. Tim Guénard, who wrote about the abuse he suffered as a child, describes the experience. "When Martine [his wife] asks me, at a particular moment, why I'm reacting oddly, I can't answer because I don't know. When I am calm again, I remember a buried wound. Talking about it soothes the wound and I can do better the next time."

Memories That Haunt Us

A person may enjoy several years of respite and then one day, out of the blue, be bombarded by an onslaught of memories he thought were locked away safely in the place where we store what we forget. I read a dialogue between two women on an Internet site dealing with that issue that moved me deeply.[8] I think they were fairly young, perhaps around thirty. I transcribed their short exchange. The first wrote,

Hello, everyone. Over the last week, childhood memories, memories I had buried for ten years, have resurfaced and won't go away. I'd like to send them back to the deepest depths of my memory, but I can't. Little by little, they are making it hard for me to enjoy life. Has anyone else had a similar experience? How do you deal with these difficult memories?

The second answered,

That happens to me sometimes too. I think it's hard to fight off those memories. Maybe you should just let them in, be strong and face up to them so you can return them to the vault. If they are coming back, there must be a reason. Maybe it's time to talk about them so that you can really and truly forget. I assume they aren't very pleasant.

Maybe you need to talk with the people who were involved, if that's still possible. Otherwise, the best thing to do is to take action when it happens. Talk, do things . . . but they often come back at night, when you're anxious and alone and would like to be able to forget the pain. I haven't found the answer yet and it's even hard for me to talk about. Over time, you can learn to handle it, especially with someone you love and who loves you. Good luck.

Beyond the pain voiced in that exchange, I am struck by the compassionate and sensible advice the second woman offered. "If these memories are coming back," she says, "there must be a reason." That is true. A memory never comes to mind without a reason. The problem is that almost any association of ideas can lead us to a memory, without our even realizing it. "Maybe it's time to talk about them so that you can really and truly forget." The central problem in addressing this kind of trauma is that, with a few exceptions, people do not find someone to really talk to (excluding therapists). Parents are not always the best candidates (or don't want to know) and friends may not be prepared to deal with the breadth of the problem. A boyfriend or girlfriend is usually not appropriate either, because revealing these wounds could put the relationship at risk. What if your partner brings up the issue during the next argument? "Maybe you need to talk about these memories with the people who were involved." Yes, that would be important. However, a traumatized person tends to think that conversation would be pointless. Who would willingly acknowledge inflicting that kind of pain? The likelier scenario is that the victim would be treated as sick or crazy and sent packing. However, even if the guilty person will not acknowledge fault, the traumatized person must shed the burden that does not belong to him. Using words to hand back the trauma the victim was forced to endure, whether the perpetrator accepts them or not, offers the victim a way to separate from and rid himself of that burden. Symbolically, it is similar to the process in which people leave their letters at my office. "Over time, you can learn to manage it, especially with someone you love and who loves you," she concludes. I have nothing to add to that. I thank this kind woman for her wonderful letter.

Trauma Victims Don't Necessarily Stand Out in a Crowd

We all have hidden stories. Behind the civility and good manners, behind the impeccable suit and tie or perfectly matched skirt-blouse-bag-and-heels and behind the corner office with a view, the men and women we meet every day carry childhood memories as fragile as crystal next to their hearts. One may have spent his childhood with an abusive father or a depraved mother; another may have come face-to-face with prison life because her mother committed a serious crime; yet another may be the child of undocumented immigrants who lived in fear and poverty resulting from their illegal status. But you can't tell by looking at them that they need our compassion. We have to be careful about drawing hasty or unfavorable impressions about another person. You may meet someone who leaves you feeling cool, another you don't find very likable and yet another you consider actively unpleasant. This person could be a grocery store clerk, a child's teacher or the friend of a friend. And because we don't like him or her, we remain distant, absent or indifferent. But experience reminds us that we never know the distances others have had to travel. How could we? We should always pay attention in case another person needs a caring gesture or a friendly word, like the woman who responded to the individual suffering from a resurgence of painful memories.

DENIAL AND SECRECY: WHEN WE DENY THE STORY, WE REJECT THE PERSON

Whether they want to or not, individuals who have been assaulted or traumatized will continue to feel the shock wave generated by the experience. Trauma is not simply the painful experience inflicted on someone, but a challenge to the victim's very existence as well. A young man hit by a car that failed to yield right of way once told me that as the car barreled toward him, he said to himself, "No, this can't be happening. Why would he want to kill me?" When trauma is involved, the "every man for himself" rule prevails as far as the guilty party is concerned. The young man said that he never saw the driver who caused the accident again. He almost lost his leg, spent months in the hospital and underwent several operations, but the driver never came to see him. The victim felt that he had been punished without ever having committed a crime. He also felt neglected, ignored and abandoned by the person responsible for it all. Until the victim consciously sets about to rebuild, he will not recover his sense of existence; the harm must be acknowledged so that the unconscious can allow life to resume.

In general, people want to forget the impacts of trauma. The aggressor wants to "forget" his guilty act as quickly as possible. The victim wants to erase the painful memory and resume his normal life as quickly as possible. People close to the victim don't know how to manage the awkward situation and the overly bright light it casts. After the initial shock, when the victim feels ready to confront the reality of his trauma, he often faces a wall of silence that family and friends erected during the period while he was "asleep." Daily life picks up. The people around him undermine his efforts to confront the issue, whether with pseudo-understanding ("Try to forget; you'll be better off that way") or by behaving as if nothing happened. Silence can have a powerful impact on the traumatized individual. As I wrote recently, a victim of incest or child sexual abuse must have an opportunity to verbalize the traumatic experience and express his continuing feelings (including affects, disgust, distress, incomprehension, hatred and a sense of injustice or failure), no matter how long ago the traumatic event occurred.[9] While incest and child sexual abuse are best treated as quickly as possible (we call it a "psychological debriefing"), it is never too late. Even decades later, clearing out the tangle of feelings and acknowledging the emotions can be useful and comforting for the victim.

Family and friends should not try to minimize what happened by saying, "It's not as bad as all that," "You shouldn't turn it into a disease," "You're still alive" or "You'll see, you'll feel better soon" or by trying to put themselves in the child's place, because that's just not possible. Rather than try to do too much, the wiser course is simply to accept what the person shares with you and offer a comforting response, like, "It must be difficult for you to talk about what happened. You are very brave."

I want to emphasize that victims of sexual abuse face a struggle that is extremely isolating. Fortunately, attitudes are changing and the walls of silence are collapsing. Parents are proud to fight to defend a child who was put in danger. The meaning of "honor" is changing too. That's all for the better.

THE MEMORY OF TRAUMA AND
THE PSYCHOTHERAPEUTIC PROCESS

Swiss psychologist Alice Miller is one of the most prolific writers on the issue of child abuse and the trauma it produces.[10] She strongly supports psychoanalytically based psychotherapy that addresses childhood issues. "Therapy should make it possible for patients to verbalize their early wounds," she writes. "We will not get very far if we try to escape the truth we are carrying within us. The denied truth will be with us wherever we flee. It will cause us pain, prompt us to do things we will regret, increase our confusion and weaken our self-confidence. But if we face up to it, we have a chance of finally recognizing what happened, what didn't happen and what has forced us to end up living our lives in opposition to our most profound needs."[11] She concurs with the work of well-respected researchers in this area, emphasizing the brain impairment that can result from early deficits with the primary caregiver. "Small children who are beaten or otherwise abused can develop lesions because . . . a condition of extreme stress can bring about the destruction of newly formed neurons and their interconnections."[12]

In such situations, she hypothesizes that the cognitive and emotional systems can collaborate and create a bridge between the two. "From my own experience, I know that this does take place in therapies systematically addressing the traumatic experiences and emotions of childhood and thus weakening those barriers in our minds. Once this has happened, it is possible to activate areas of the brain not hitherto drawn upon, presumably for fear of the pain and distress that recalling earlier instances of abuse would arouse."[13]

Wounds of the past engraved long ago on the brain do not simply disappear as if by magic. The goal of psychotherapy is not to harass an individual by returning continuously to the issue of early childhood trauma, but to provide an opportunity to confront, rather than flee, reality, take the experience seriously and analyze the remaining connections to that past so that the individual can be freed from it.

The memory of trauma is paradoxical. On the one hand, the individual must forget the memory to relieve his suffering and be redirected toward tolerable, if not normal, ways of life. On the other, he must remember because the trauma endured will always be part of his larger psychic structure. It will be part of him.

Certain forms of suffering and personal affliction are so powerful that they call for a monument to the memories, like cities that erect monuments to the war dead. Unfortunately we don't build monuments to isolated, traumatized individuals, who must construct their tomb deep in their hearts.

It is difficult to talk about trauma and victims of trauma. Individuals who have lived through highly stressful periods or have experienced shock do not necessarily appreciate the compassion of normal—nontraumatized—people. The situation requires us to simply accept the traumatized individual's words rather than offer pity or pretend to understand. Ultimately we are all victims of the trauma associated with birth, as Austrian psychologist Otto Rank noted.[14] We are all potential trauma victims, whether directly or as perpetrators or witnesses. We must live with that suffering.

The decision to revisit a painful past is always sensitive. The relief we hope to gain must be worth the risk.

CHAPTER 11

Memories and Guilt

If we can interpret his childhood, youth and history
so that a fairly concrete (and promising) path
emerges, he will no longer experience his past
as an unbearable burden, but as a point of departure
leading to a more reasonable future.
—JOSEF RATTNER, *DIE KUNST:*
EINE LEBENGESCHICHTE ZU LESEN

IT DOESN'T TAKE MUCH TO TURN
A PERSON'S LIFE UPSIDE DOWN

We often talk about acts of aggression or violence committed by adults, but we rarely mention those committed by children. I assume that this results from a certain taboo. We prefer to think of children as innocent cherubs, not miniature adults who may be indifferent, nasty or violent. I hesitated before using the word "commit" in the first sentence because it seemed a bit harsh applied to children. While I do not place children and adults in the

same category or accuse children of gratuitous violence, tyranni-
cal behavior or barbaric acts, children who live in an adult world
and witness adult behavior may be tempted to copy adult behavior, just as they, like adults, are exposed to the vicissitudes and
the unknowns of fate.

We were all children once and have all experienced situations in which the slightest action could have turned life upside
down. And while the cherub is always there to tug on our heart-
strings, the incorrigible little wild animal is always close by, too.
Of course, the little wild animal doesn't exist. That's an adult
view of the world. Children rarely judge other children. Judgment remains the prerogative of adults. They're the ones who
label people. (Take a quick look at teachers' comments on report
cards and you'll understand what I mean.)

CHILDHOOD IS NOT ALL ROSY

We all have our hidden childhood stories, and we're not necessarily proud of them. The low blows, betrayals, revenge, small
acts of viciousness and transgressions that occur during childhood leave a bitter taste. When a child gives in to them, he
seemingly abandons the blissful weightlessness of innocence for
the chaotic road of life. Hermann Hesse describes that state perfectly in the beginning of his novel *Demian*. Emil Sinclair is a little boy torn between two worlds. His parents' is upright, tidy and
filled with light, while the other world is dark and shady. He can
sense its existence in the servants' conversation and the chatter
among children at the local school. During one of his escapades,
he meets Frantz Kromer, the son of a tailor, a "robust and brutal"

boy who is just thirteen, but whose adult behavior impresses Emil. Not to be outdone by his friends, he becomes tangled in a series of lies that Frantz uses to blackmail him. Suddenly Emil's life is turned upside down. Hesse's gift is his ability to describe this passage from innocent cherub to child who thinks his world is lost forever. "But all of it was lost to me now, all of it belonged to the clear, well-lighted world of my father and mother, and I, guilty and deeply engulfed in an alien world, was entangled in adventures and sin, threatened by an enemy—by dangers, fear and shame . . . My feet had become muddied, I could not even wipe them clean on the mat."[1]

Emil Sinclair did not lie out of malice. He wanted to look powerful in the other children's eyes, so he told a story about stealing apples from an orchard but became tangled in a web of complicated explanations. Pieced together, they gradually formed the image of a corrupt child with whom he would now have to learn to coexist.

Unhappy childhood memories always have an element of fatality. Stories of paradise, hell, purgatory and sin remind us that we are fallible at every moment.

Our Culture's "Logic of Guilt"

Guilt has a long history in Western societies. Cain and Abel, Adam and Eve, Christ dying for our sins and the Ten Commandments are among the references that have helped anchor a sense of guilt in our hearts. Thanks to the messages society transmits through school systems and parental authority, we are well prepared to live in a culture of guilt and, in particular, self-guilt. We are guilty in the eyes of God, our parents and the other. Every person must look inside himself to uncover his past and present sins. Transgressions, lies, breaches, opportunism and domination are considered serious flaws in education and upbringing, and religion considers them sins. However, in their own lives, adults see them as simple failings.

This combination of social instruction ("No one is above the law"), religious instruction ("You must repent and perform an act of contrition") and parental instruction ("It serves you right," "It's your fault," "If you had only. . .") produces a logic of guilt. As a result, the child always feels guilty of something, even if she's done nothing wrong (the fear of the policeman), thereby setting in motion what Milan Kundera calls the "culpabilization" machine, a reflex that persists into adulthood.

The weight of guilt is always difficult to bear. One way to lighten it is to seek comfort in unconscious mechanisms. Some people look outside, to beliefs and superstitions, for reasons that explain their misfortune, as expressed in thoughts like, "I should've expected this," "I'll have to pay for this," "It's my karma," and "It's my just reward." This is common and should be interpreted as a projection of guilt, as psychologist Carole Damiani confirms in an article about treating traumatized individuals. "The subject will only gradually be able to give meaning to the event and his experience," she explains. "The construction of meaning will occur by developing a feeling of guilt, which originates in the individual history. The subject may interpret the pain as a fundamental injustice or on the contrary, as just punishment for a misdeed, whether real or imaginary."[2]

The critical issue with respect to criminal acts to which we are exposed as children seems to be the "sting of conscience" we continue to feel. A woman recently told me that as a child, her brother set fire to an abandoned chicken coop in their backyard. When her father ran outside, barefoot, to put out the flames, he stepped on a rusty nail. That was the end of the incident. I assume that her brother got a pretty harsh talking to. But if things had ended in tragedy, what effect would that have had on the boy? For example, what if the father had ignored the wound and died of tetanus? Objectively, it wasn't the child's fault that the father ran outside barefoot, and he wasn't responsible for the rusty nail on the ground. Nonetheless, we can imagine the sense of guilt that child would have been exposed to.

Children's actions are often thoughtless. From one perspective, they may be minor but from another, they can turn nightmarish, as they did for Emil Sinclair. It all depends on the context, the nature of the act and, in particular, each person's perspective.

Children can commit a host of negligent actions that adults may consider reprehensible, including everything related to sex. Playing doctor is a normal game that millions of children, boys and girls, engage in at the age of three, four and five. However, in light of recent pedophilia scandals, we see this differently now and may react in an extreme way to such incidents. Psychotherapists occasionally see families who have been completely undone, if not destroyed, because their little boy wanted to show his peepee to the little girl next door (or vice versa). It can be difficult, on your own, to evaluate a child's thoughtless action.

BERNARD FELT THE WEIGHT
OF GUILT FOR MANY YEARS

Bernard, a bookseller, came to see me after a coworker said to him casually, "So are you a repressed type?" He smiled, without really understanding, but the remark hit him in the stomach because he sensed that it was true at some level. Bernard felt that he had always carried a weight. Everything was fine at times, but at others he found life very difficult. During those moments, he had a hard time concentrating, working and being available to other people. He described himself as fairly cool toward others, but said that he had a close circle of friends and considered himself an open person. His personal life was all right, although he didn't have a girlfriend at the moment. Sex was not a simple matter for him. He said he had some problems, which he did not describe. The rest of the session went smoothly. I explained what psychotherapy involves and what the patient can expect. He made an appointment for the following week.

When he came back, he began by saying, "I know what my problem is but it's too hard for me to talk about." I told him that if that was the case, he didn't have to discuss it and could wait until he was comfortable addressing the issue. That leeway gave him the courage to open up. "Twenty-two years ago, I engaged in sexual touching with my two sisters," he said. "I was ten but I haven't stopped thinking about it since. With my older sister, she was the one who started it. We were on vacation, sleeping in bunk beds. One night she said to me, 'Do you want to touch me down there? Wait until I'm asleep.'" Bernard went into her bed and did what she asked. Another time, she told one of the little boys to go into her room with her. Bernard stayed with his eight-year-old sister and showed her his penis. The little sister did not seem to be particularly traumatized and did not cry. Later, however, Bernard found the situation he had initiated to be very painful. While he and his older sister had been equally wrong, he said, he was the guilty party in the episode involving his younger sister. I asked him if he and she had talked about it later. No, he answered, that would have been impossible. He would've been too ashamed.

Based on his explanation, I did not find the incident particularly serious. Many children play similar games. I suggested that he open up to his sister to relieve the pressure he had felt for more than twenty years. He seemed to have decided to do so, but at the next session he told me that he had not found the right moment. At the same time, he was aware that it bothered him terribly.

At the next session, he told me that he had finally spoken to his sister. "I was pretty anxious on the way over to see her," he said. "I was in a daze. I told her that if I had hurt her, I wanted to ask her to forgive me. We talked about it for an hour. She told me that she had never felt traumatized but was really pleased that I talked about it. She had tried to but never quite dared. It was amazing. From the expression on her face, I could tell how happy she was that I would open up to her like that." During the conversation, she told him that she'd always considered him a role model. She added that he had given her the best gift a woman could have asked for. (By coincidence, their conversation took place on International Women's Day.) "It's as if we rediscovered each other," he said. "As if other things have opened up. Now I think I'll be able to enjoy life and be happy. I'll be able to break down other barriers, like saying 'I love you' to a girl."

Because we hear so many sordid stories of sexual abuse with awful endings, this one may seem somewhat surprising. Haunted by the traumatizing memory, Bernard bore that weight for twenty-two years. Verbalizing it, first with a psychotherapist and then with his sister, relieved him of it.

There are no rules when it comes to trauma. Each person's sensitivity will determine the significance or seriousness of the event. At a different age or under different circumstances, another little girl might have experienced the same event as a genuine trauma. And similarly, another little boy could have interpreted it as just "playing doctor."

Do We Have to Live with Our Mistakes?

The wounds that one child inflicts on another are usually minor and without real consequences. They generally involve some stupid behavior that gets out of hand. However, a child may cause, witness, be responsible for or be guilty of causing other injuries and suffering that are experienced as traumatic events. For example, how would a child feel who accidentally (I could also say "was responsible for," but that would be too accusatory) knocked over a pot of boiling water on his little sister or pushed his brother out of a tree, leaving him disabled? What memory would follow that child throughout childhood and into adulthood? None of us can avoid the pain of remorse, and we experience it each time our conscience revisits the action (or failure to take action) that produced the mistake. That part of the past is bound tightly to us and we must learn to live with it. "What if I hadn't done this or that?" "What if I hadn't said this or that?" "What if I'd arrived two seconds earlier?" "Or if I'd reacted right away?" Those endless questions bring us back, over and over again, to a past we can do nothing to change but that continues to pursue us.

When an accident occurs, we are usually concerned about the victim, which is normal. The victim's medical, emotional and even psychological needs are treated, as they should be. But the person who is responsible—the one who faces the pointing fingers—also needs somewhere to lay down his burdens, from his psychological suffering to his guilty conscience, regret and remorse, especially when that person is a child.

THE VICTIM'S SENSE OF GUILT

Bernard's case showed how hard it was for him to bear the burden of a fault he considered unforgivable. What is really astounding is when the victim, not the aggressor, develops guilt feelings. Several factors come into play in this process, including educational, social and religious ones. Popular morality always takes a guarded view of interpersonal conflicts (between two people), as if both individuals played a part. While a group attack on an individual is clearly acknowledged as a traumatic event, an individual attack on another individual may be viewed suspiciously, as if there might be a question as to who was the attacker and who the victim. Someone will always ask, directly or indirectly, whether one person provoked the other, as if to suggest a legitimate reason for the aggression. Until recently, for example, society, including the police, responded with a smirk to women who charged harassment, sexual abuse or rape because they were suspected of having somehow provoked their attack. Comments like, "Did you see how she was dressed? She was asking for it!" suggest the public's willingness to reverse the roles and rail against the victim rather than the victimizer.

Experiencing guilt after a traumatic event reflects a well-known psychological mechanism. To paraphrase Freud, it involves (varying degrees of) self-criticism that seeks to hold the self responsible for the trauma. Just as we project our own weaknesses onto others, we tend to project, or "introject," the weaknesses of others onto ourselves. The question is why. Writer Milan Kundera offers an interesting response to the question of guilt. Reflecting on Dostoevsky's *Crime and Punishment* and Kafka's *The Trial,* he speaks of a reverse logic. Raskolnikov committed a crime, Kundera explains, but unable to bear the burden of his guilt, he agrees to be punished so that he can be at peace with himself. "It's the well-known situation where the offense seeks the punishment," Kundera says. "In Kafka, the logic is reversed. The person punished does not know the reason for the punishment. The absurdity of the punishment is so unbearable that to find peace, the accused needs to find a justification for his penalty: the punishment seeks the offense."[3]

I believe that trauma involves the same reverse logic. The victim is so shaken that to relieve the anguish which comes from being punished for no reason, she would rather assume the guilt than accept the absurdity of her situation. The logic is illogical, but we always prefer tortured logic to no logic. The Harold Ramis movie *Analyze This* offers a perfect illustration. Of course, the film's success owed more to the comic situation than to the story, given that until Tony Soprano showed up at a psychiatrist's office, no one had heard of a depressed Mafia boss. Still, it is lovely and touching.

THE CASE OF PAUL VITTI

Analyze This is the story of a painful trauma that the hero, Paul Vitti (Robert De Niro), experienced as a child. Thirty-five years later, the trauma manifests through symptoms that are incompatible with the life of a Mafia godfather, including anxiety attacks, crying jags, emotional blocks, fits of guilt and hypersensitivity. Vitti consults a psychiatrist, Ben Sobel (Billy Crystal), which leads to the psychological process known as transference (and countertransference). The psychiatrist acts as an emotional "midwife," helping Vitti recover the traumatic images so that he can be released from them and healed of his symptoms.

When he was ten, Vitti and his parents were in a restaurant. A busboy approached the table and shot his father. Vitti had sensed that something was wrong before the shot was fired. Moments earlier, his father had been furious with him, leaving the child unable to respond ("Because of his anger, I couldn't get a word out," he says in the film.) In that moment, the gangster had enough time to pull the trigger. Here's the dialogue:

> *You blame yourself.*
> *I, I could've saved him.*
> *But you were mad.*
> *I should've said something.*
> *You couldn't have saved him.*
> *I killed him.*
> *You didn't kill him, Paul. You didn't kill him. You were mad at him, but that was the life he chose.*
> *I let him die. I couldn't say good-bye to him.*

This exchange illustrates how the child internalized the wound linked to the loss of his father, killed before his eyes, and how Paul's unconscious created two categories of feelings, one superimposed on the other. The message goes like this: because I was angry at my father for subjecting me to his rages, I am responsible for his death. Eventually Vitti even says that he let his father die and then that he killed him. In a full-bore psychodramatic production, Vitti regresses to childhood, unleashing his emotions and identifying the psychiatrist as his father. Calling him "Dad," Vitti pours out all the feelings and words he had held back for years.

> *Why don't you say it now, Paul? If he was here, what would you say to him?*
> *I can't, I can't. I want to say, "I'm sorry, Dad. I'm so sorry, Dad." I let him down . . .*

You couldn't have saved him, Paul.
I could have.

The psychiatrist then tries to reconstruct Vitti's narcissistic image and help him sublimate the loss of his father. "He was trying to save you. That's what you fought about. He didn't want this for you."

Finally he offers Vitti a way to rebuild a meaningful present and future life by talking to him about his own son. "And you don't want this for Anthony. You don't want him to grow up the way you did, without a father."

The psychiatrist's final message is almost spiritual. "Your father's not dead, Paul. He's alive in you. And he's trying to tell you something."

Granted, we're talking about a movie here, with its compromises, shortcuts and fast-forwards. However, it is important to emphasize that a person traumatized in childhood can suppress the trauma for years, that a simple incident or event can reactivate it and how, once recalled, it can prove redemptive and create a sense of promise for the future if the memory is worked through properly (in psychotherapy, for example).

We know this because we have all experienced it to some degree. Our vision of human existence and the behaviors that follow from it are based on our life experiences. We have all felt the different weight of happiness and sadness and good and evil at least once. We know that ten positive experiences do not make up for a single painful one. Our childhood mistakes follow that path too. A child's life is a series of experiences that teach her where she fits in the world and how to correct her mistakes. That life will naturally include missteps, errors, bad habits, transgressions and actions that warrant varying degrees of criticism and even blame. Our life takes a certain direction and not another because we experienced a particular event, under particular circumstances, with particular parents. All lived experience, subjective and objective, courses through memories of trauma. Human life is not compartmentalized. We do not move systematically from one delimited stage of life to another, from childhood to adolescence to adulthood. Like a puzzle piece, every life experience has a place somewhere in the gradual process of assembling the whole.

Discovering your history through your childhood memories can be painful. Unfortunately, fleeing it can hurt even more, both consciously and unconsciously. People will tell you not to go digging around in the past for fear of uncovering disturbing information. They're right and wrong. When we rearrange the furniture, we may stir up some dust, but we may also find some old papers or important objects we had thought were lost forever. Discovering your history is always worth the trouble.

CHAPTER 12

Memories Have a Therapeutic Function

Our life is a journey
Through winter and night
We look for our way
In a sky without light.
—LOUIS-FERDINAND CELINE,
SONG OF THE SWISS GUARDS:
JOURNEY TO THE END OF THE NIGHT

MEMORIES, PERSONAL HISTORY AND SELF-IMAGE

The ordinary person knows very little about himself unless he is involved in long-term psychotherapy or psychoanalysis. This may be difficult to accept, but most of what we know about ourselves and how we evaluate that knowledge comes from other people, not from our own self-reflection. Nietzsche said, "Each man is furthest from himself." Sociologist Michel Juffé expands on the idea. "We know who we are only because someone has told us. Told, that is, and not merely signified or signaled by gestures and attitudes. And we are what we are in the way it was said and, perhaps, all the more by whom it was said."[1] Most of what we perceive about ourselves thus comes from our parents and other adults close to us, which brings us back to what is stored in our memories.

Our memories are the manifestation of what I call our "sense of historicity," or how we integrate the continuum of our past, present and future into our present life. (I consider this an indicator of mental health.) It is probably more accurate to say, as Juffé does, that the kinds of relationships we had with those closest to us every day has the most powerful influence on our memories and the kinds of memories we developed, whether positive, negative, distressing or painful. For example, if a single mother with alcohol problems loses interest in her child, fails to provide parental support and prevents him from developing normal relationships with peers by forbidding him to spend time with friends and participate in activities, the child will likely learn to withdraw. His childhood memories will bear the mark of that solitude and absence of affection. To take another example, if a woman gives birth to an unwanted baby, that child may experience the entire family's silent disapproval throughout childhood. This is what happened to Kathrin, a young woman who recently started psychotherapy. We had several difficult but wonderful sessions on that issue and she agreed to allow me to describe parts of them.

KATHRIN: LIVING IN A NEW LAND

Kathrin told me that while she was on vacation at her parents' house in Germany, she suddenly felt a strong and upsetting sense of shame that she had experienced in the past. "As a child, I was the little girl who wasn't supposed to be there," she explained. "I was not a wanted child. My birth certificate read, 'father unknown.' I was the family's source of shame so I became ashamed of my existence and had to hide. We never discussed the issue within the family and I never dared to ask my mother about it. She avoided it too. Even today, she never talks to me about my childhood. That hurts.

"This summer, I had that feeling of shame at being alive again. It was strange, as if I were looking for my childhood. I stared at everything, questioningly—other people, my mother, places. Even looking at photographs of my mother from my childhood made me feel ashamed. I examined them closely. Did she look happy? Unhappy ? I felt like I was on the brink of tears all day.

"I have had this feeling in the past, but this time I realized, from the outside, that my childhood had always been like this. At that point, I understood (I think the psychotherapy helped) why I had become such an expert at forgetting. Whenever something troubling came up in my life, it couldn't be discussed or even considered. You had to act as if nothing had happened. You just wiped it all away and started over again. Now I understand that that's how I ended up moving from Germany to France. It was absolutely perfect for me. I underestimated myself throughout my entire childhood. I had no self-confidence. At one point, while traveling in Italy, I met a boy who lived in Monaco. All I could think about was moving there. Moving to France was like being reborn. I quickly gained a new sense of self-confidence, made friends and found a job. The most surprising thing was how quickly I learned French. Everyone was amazed by my accent."

After Kathrin took a moment to compose herself, I explained that leaving everything behind can also be a way to forget. I thought of a passage in one of my books, which I read to her.[2]

> *To leave, not to flee, but to go elsewhere, where life's predicaments are less complicated, daily existence simpler and worries less burdensome.*
>
> *To leave, not to conquer another El Dorado, but finally to live in harmony with oneself, with all those images we have of ourselves; images that we never express and allow to breathe, but silence, distort and sacrifice because if we really were all those images that we hold close to our heart, we would be ashamed of our own beauty.*
>
> *To leave, still oneself even as we become another, because changing horizons means coming to know other landscapes, people, customs and, thus, growing as we encounter all those elsewheres along the way.*
>
> *To leave, to no longer belong, to shed our everyday identity and, finally, become a full person because a*

stranger, without past, without restraints, without nar-
row mindedness, without family ties, without any bag-
gage at all.

I waited a few moments because I could see that both of us were deeply moved. I then explained that leaving, turning away from one's birthplace, roots and language—even one's accent—can be a useful way to banish a memory. Which memory? That of an absent father who could have given her legitimacy. Living in a new land often allows us to discover another self whose existence was previously unknown. I had that profound experience when I lived in Berlin. At the same time, I felt strongly that mother and daughter loved each other very much, so I encouraged Kathrin to address that and talk with her mother about that part of their life. This is particularly important because our past tends to catch up with us just when we want to flee it, and Kathrin's children were starting to ask questions about her early life.

The history of our childhood relationships shapes and molds our identity and continues to do so throughout life. A father who disappeared without leaving an address or died too young, an unstable mother, a grandfather with a prison record, an alcoholic uncle or an older sister with a serious illness—these people are the worries we take on as ours during childhood. They require us to position and reposition ourselves continuously, even when we reach adulthood, because our most important concern will always be knowing what we are worth to other people. How can we present them the most favorable image of ourselves? In other words, do others see me as a good person? This concern influences much of our behavior. Regardless of social environment or age, we all need that reassurance. Likewise, we all ask the same question, whether we admit it or not: How can I convince others to think well of me?

Our past experiences and the childhood memories of them are the emotional foundation on which we build this image and, through it, our identity. Human beings endure repudiation, betrayal, abandonment and permanent states of violence. These are some of the accidents of life that most of us struggle against to preserve or restore an image of ourselves that we are willing to let others see.

YESTERDAY'S CHILD CAN HEAL TODAY'S ADULT

Memories may hamper our development by narrowing our cognitive horizon and trapping us in a narrow perception of ourselves and our existence. However, their living, dynamic structure can also expand our lives in unexpected ways. When we manage to avoid the trap of working the same ground over and over, move beyond the dangerous shoals of our traumatic memories and succeed in bringing other images to the surface—just as we manage to recall a name on the tip of our tongue—then unexpected chapters of our life, childhood and past will reappear. Images, words, secrets, sensations and scents will rise up from some unknown depth. We cannot even say we had forgotten them; rather, we simply left them on the side of the road because we had to tend to the essential, to pushing ahead, growing up without too much damage and building a shield to protect against pain.

To achieve that, we must conquer our resistance and abandon our tired ideas and myths about ourselves ("I am condemned to live this way, this is my fate, I don't deserve anything better. . ."). We must be brave enough to believe that something else exists within us, in our head, heart and gut, something other than these wounds we have known since childhood. We must also be brave enough to believe that there is more to the human spirit than childhood's painful memories. Other memories—thousands, millions of other memories—exist within us, prepared to emerge as soon as we signal our readiness. They are powerful enough to heal the others. Memories will come back, followed by other unexpected and surprising ones. They will take their place in our conscious life, as if yesterday's child were returning to do the job properly this time. Today's adult may suffer for yesterday's child, but only that child can heal the adult's heart and reconcile it with life, others, children, parents and the important adults in his life who may have deceived, betrayed, rejected or acted with violence against him.

I like to say that love heals love. It sounds simple, but it is difficult to put into practice. That's normal. When we are bewitched, almost hypnotized, by love, we refuse to let it go. But when a new love appears, we see how quickly the heart's wounds heal, in spite of ourselves and even our efforts to fight that healing. Our memories captivate us, just as images of love absorb and hypnotize us. They are the photographs of our childhood and we look back at them when we are in doubt or in need. We come back to them often. However, like all photographs, they capture a frozen image of our life and limit its scope, diverting energy from our present existence, as if we were constantly returning to places we know well but abandoned long ago.

Just as love heals love, memories heal memories. They play a therapeutic role because as they are expressed more fully, they release a huge amount of trapped life energy. By remembering and verbalizing our childhood memories, we also learn to see them in a different and fuller light. By restructuring the individual's world of memories, the psychotherapist guides him to see them from another perspective, look at them differently and distinguish among them. This process requires us to dismantle the Self that we constructed (that exists in opposition to our true self) so that we can face life, the other and ourselves, even as we reorganize our general perception of ourselves and life. That is why so many people compare psychotherapy to being reborn.

Our memories make up our primary references to our life experience. Strangely, the known is always less frightening than the unknown, even when it includes tragic aspects. As a result, people make personal or professional choices that conflict with the happiness they could experience. We call this the phenomenon of repetition. Contrary to what you might think, most people understand this fairly well. One day, a young woman told me, in a tone intended to be humorous, about her determination to loosen the stranglehold that was suffocating her. "When I was seven, I decided to leave my true self in a safe place and live through my double. I was always playing a role." However, she had met a man who made her very happy and she loved him very much. She wanted to start a new life with him, decided that she'd had enough of this self-exile and could no longer accept her own deception. "I don't want to live in a state of oblivion anymore," she said. "I want to live as the person I really am. I want to leave this double behind and reconnect with my real self. I want to be a regular woman, with all a regular woman's flaws and qualities." We may invent someone we are not and create a personality that does not belong to us, but one day we will have to leave appearances behind, seek our true self and discover our history. To do that, we must set out in search of our true self. From that moment, no one else—other people, society or even you—will be able to program that self to "function perfectly," in social or emotional terms (or will at least exercise only a minimum of control). To the extent possible, this self will live a straightforward and authentic life, a life that draws on its own energy and life spirit.

Part Five

*Discovering
Your History*

CHAPTER 13

Your Three Childhood Memories

This past . . . is not a set of events over there, at a
distance from me, but the atmosphere of my present.
—MAURICE MERLEAU-PONTY,
PHENOMENOLOGY OF PERCEPTION

WHERE WE STARTED, WHERE WE'VE COME

Let's take a moment to review. We began with Freud's and Adler's contributions, focusing on Adler's productive tools for analyzing childhood memories. Next, we took a theoretical detour to better understand how what we remember and what we forget are inscribed in memory processes. Perhaps you found that part of the book slow going, as it is rather dense. We then analyzed the gradual formation of family relationships, beginning with the infant-mother and infant-father (or the infant-father-mother) relationship and then incorporating the relationships with other family members. Building on this theoretical base, I then showed you how we can draw valuable information about the role of the mother-father-child core nuclear relationship, as well as information on the role of the other "active components" of memories, like place, time, objects, animals and emotions from three childhood memories. After covering the principle of core nuclear relationships, I then addressed the importance of the principle of outwardly directed movement in our childhood memories and its key role in shaping our perception of our internal world, the external world and others. To illustrate, I sketched out my childhood memories, using the process of interpretation that I recommend. Last, I discussed the emotional wounds that childhood memories express and showed you how our unconscious seeks to manage them.

The technique for analyzing three memories that I outlined in Part 3 provides a set of unique tools that can help you understand how you relate simultaneously to yourself, your personality, style of life and, as a result, others. When we learn to identify the basis for our actions and behaviors, we also begin to recognize the sources of our limitations, failings, difficulties and problems, as well as our abilities, aptitudes and inclinations.

Now let's return to the three memories you wrote down and take a look at what they tell you. Since I'm not actually sitting there with you, I will let you select the issues you want to analyze as we work through our tool box. If you performed the exercise at the beginning of the book, you will have three very useful memories and will be able to address them productively.

How Did You React to
My Request for Your Memories?

Before we continue, please think back to what prompted you to pick up this book. Were you just curious? Does psychology fascinate you? Did the title appeal? Did it carry some sense of mystery? Did it speak to experiences or feelings you've been living with for a long time? Did you choose it because you hoped it might lift a burden you have borne since childhood?

The next issue addresses your reaction to my request to write down your recollections. If you have a good memory, you will recall that I said we'd come back to that because some of you may have been staring at a big black hole or were unable to come up with a memory you thought was important enough to put down on paper. Now ask yourself how it felt to dive into those memories. Were you eager to participate in the exercise? Did you resist? Did you ask yourself whether there might be a trap somewhere? Did you try to figure out where the book was going? The response to these very general questions will help you understand your overall ability to cooperate or your tendency toward distrust or resistance. It will also help you understand your general state of mind about your memories. We should always be aware of that state of mind as we embark on an activity because it colors our experiences.

When I see patients, I pay careful attention to a person's reaction when I ask for memories. That reaction offers the psychotherapist a wealth of information. First, it speaks to the individual's relationship to her past. Does she have many memories or just a few? Does she enjoy thinking about and remembering them? The reaction also tells us about the person's emotional sensitivity to the unexpected. Is she surprised? Worried? Does she respond with her own questions? The reaction also offers insight into an individual's tendency to open up to others. Does she share her memories easily, naturally, simply and generously or does she have a hard time expressing them? The person's first words are revealing in this context too. She may say, "A childhood memory? What kind of memory?" "I don't know, nothing comes to mind immediately" or "I'll have to think about it, I never gave it much thought." That kind of response expresses resistance or holding back. Conversely, other people turn out to be surprisingly long-winded. You have to ask them to slow down so that you can organize and keep track of what they are saying. They seem to glow at the very idea of remembering. The internal smile that is part of their memory lights up their face. You sense that they are burning with impatience to share those moments with you.

I found it very difficult to interpret the memories I recounted at the beginning of the book. Something in me was blocked and I had to start over several times. All of a sudden, I would have nothing else to say, my examples seemed trite and I was convinced that readers would be bored by what I had to say. I was sure about one thing—talking about my own memories would expose me. I decided to put off the interpretation until I felt more comfortable opening myself up to you. Finally, several weeks later, while riding a bus from São Paulo to Ouro Preto, Brazil, my resistance dissolved and the words came to me.

When resistance is strong, we cannot perceive reality clearly and simply. Sometimes we need to make several attempts before we can draw a reliable picture of our experience. This applies to both our actions in life and what we retain in our memories. The more difficult the experience, the likelier the unconscious is to suppress it, find a way to avoid it and transform it into something relatively acceptable. Freud and his screen memories showed what the unconscious can do.

HOW TO APPROACH
YOUR CHILDHOOD MEMORIES

Before you proceed to an in-depth analysis of your three (or perhaps four) memories, make sure that you are comfortable and out of range of diversions (radio, television, telephone or street noise) and distractions. Put yourself in a receptive state of mind so that you will be able to accept whatever comes into your mind without resisting. I assume that you are at home, so look around and observe your environment. Note all the memory objects. You'll remember that I pointed out many of mine earlier in the book. (It would be interesting to analyze why they are present in my environment, but that would take me too far afield.) You should do the same. Make a list of them and look for the common denominator. Mine come from trips that I, or people close to me, have taken. That's at least one common denominator. What categories do your memory objects belong to? Are they books, paintings, ashtrays, records, jewelry, or simply photographs? The answer to that question alone may provide information about what you are attached to. There's another important preliminary question: Are you "Mr. Memories" (or "Ms. Memories")? Do you feel a strong pull toward the past? Do you live in the past? These questions may help you understand the extent to which you have managed to shed the residues of childhood or whether you have yet to "cut the cord" completely.

Now let's take a close look at your three memories. How old were you? I asked you to write three or four memories from early childhood—from birth to five. Do yours date from that age range or were they from five to ten? These answers will provide information about the fluidity and "livingness" (quality of energy or vigor) of your life story. If we cannot recall any early childhood memories at a particular moment, that's because our unconscious chooses to hold them back for reasons that we don't understand but that make sense to the unconscious. You will probably notice that your memories can time-travel. I'm referring to life after birth, but other experts are prepared to discuss life before birth and even prior lives. While such speculation interests me intellectually, I am not prepared to go that far.

Childhood memories often relate to specific events that may involve a (possibly traumatic) break or renewal, including a move, separation from parents, the mother or father's work-related problems or the birth of a sibling. It will be interesting to hear to what these landmark events have to say.

THE CORE NUCLEAR RELATIONSHIP
PRINCIPLE IN MEMORIES

For convenience, I will use the term "nuclearity" to refer to the family, social and environmental structure that appears in your memories. Unless otherwise indicated, this term refers to everything covered in Chapters 5 and 6.

The Presence of Nuclearity in Your Memories

If you are a "Mr. Memories" or "Ms. Memories," your three memories will likely include a classic form of nuclearity. Similarly, if you did not know your parents (if they died around the time of your birth, for example), the classic structure of core nuclearity will not appear, although it may have developed in another form (with your adoptive parents, for example).

Take a look at your three memories. Do your mother, father, brothers and sisters, grandparents and members of the extended family appear in order or out of order? Does one person have a greater presence than another? Or does just one person appear? Rather than ask why your father appears in all three and your mother in none, for example, ask why the latter is absent. There are usually good reasons. First, the positive ones. If the parent of the opposite sex is present, that may simply indicate a somewhat stronger but still classic oedipal involvement. However, a disproportionate presence could also signal lack of affection, conflict or irreconcilable hatred for a mother who was particularly cold, severe, intransigent or cruel ("My mother never loved me," "She always preferred my brother" or "There was only enough love for my father").[1] I refer here to the mother, but the individual concerned could be any close family member. If you come from a large family, this may also refer to a brother or sister closest to you.

When Nuclearity Does Not Appear

If nuclearity does not appear in orderly fashion in your memories, take a close look at who is present: an adult with a particularly strong tie (uncle, aunt or often a godfather or godmother) or a person outside the immediate family and "parafamily" circle, like a close family friend, minister, teacher, baby-sitter or neighbor. This may show how, as a child, you managed to avoid the potentially traumatic impact of a parent's actions by refocusing your emotions on that person, whom Boris Cyrulnik would call the "guardian." In dealing with memories, I like to say that the land belongs to the one who works it.

Memories That Relate to the Other Primary Components

If you review just the items presented above, you will be able to draw out some very meaningful points. Recall the section dealing with animals, which have a unique ability to give and receive affection. In certain circumstances, they can play the role of therapist. If your childhood memories involve primarily animals, you may want to ask yourself about the relationships you establish and maintain today with humans.

To take another example, you now know that memories of place express a strong need for roots. If that concerns you, you may want to think about your need for reassurance and stability. (It could be interesting to relate those memories to ones that deal with moving from place to place, which we will come to in a moment.) An emphasis on the past may express a sense of insecurity that needs to be eased by strong temporal references or feelings of nostalgia. Refugees to the United States from Bosnia or Central America, for example, might find very strong markers for place (related to a sense of exile) and time (a lost childhood), corresponding to the childhood years in their home country and the trauma of the separation.

Memories of Objects

These memories often conceal a host of information that may not be apparent at first glance. Memories of objects are not generally linked to a specific experience. As I mentioned, they often appear in the form of "flashes" or images, rather than as events that can be recounted, which makes them difficult to interpret. Memories of objects that lack connections to human beings or the world of relationships, which I call "unmediated," are quite rare. When we do encounter them, they reveal a barren internal landscape that may suggest a semiautistic condition. All memories refer to a relationship with the world, although it can be difficult to establish that connection, so we must look for the underlying symbolic or allegorical form. If you remember a set of blocks that someone gave you, for example, even if the only social representation present in the memory is that "someone," you will still recognize the underlying relationship. A medium—the gift—existed and connected you to the world of others. If you remember just a living room lamp, even if no social connection seems to emerge, we can see the lamp as a source of light and the living room as a gathering place. Fortunately, memories of objects are not reduced to such a simple message. Most of the time, they have something to say and say it well. The fireplace refers to the home; the table, to meals; the pen, to reading and writing; a file folder, to things we care about and want to keep; the refrigerator, to food; a bottle of milk, to nourishment; a fence, to an obstacle or private property. Let your mind assign the images that arise spontaneously to your memories of objects and you'll see that you're probably right.

Memories That Relate to the Senses and the Emotions

Memories related to the senses and the emotions provide information on the world of perceptions—sensory and sensual—in which you organize your life. They concern everything related to the body, including physical experiences and their expression (bodily sensations, movements, physical dynamic as well as the physical experience of femaleness and maleness, intimacy and libido), and everything related to the "heart," the emotions (including joy, pain, humor and sadness) and affective states like anger, resentment and jealousy. They address the sensory-based relationship you maintain with the world, life and your choices. This complex cocktail is a blend of your genetic heritage, physical constitution, mental and psychological processes, identity and personality, what you inherit and what you acquire—everything that is most alive in you. Childhood memories richest in elements that involve the senses and the emotions reveal the most about your "livingness," the active, responsive, energetic, engaged and passionate side of your personality.

Trauma-Related Memories

I addressed this topic at length earlier, so I won't revisit it in detail. I will simply emphasize the surprising fact that information about trauma does not appear systematically in the three memories. While we might assume they are held back out of modesty, that's not the case. Memories are more often linked to the current state of the individual's life than to the trauma-related emotions and feelings. If he is experiencing a painful, difficult or problematic period, trauma will color his memories. If, however, his life is pleasant and active, he will tend to seek out memories reflecting that state of mind. If an element of trauma appears in your memories, confirm whether it might mask a more general and immediate sense of existential weakness or inferiority.

As you can see, the relationships within and among the core components of our memories form a subtle but legible mosaic. When you evaluate and "read" them using my categories, you should obtain a considerable amount of information about your tendencies, style of life and life choices. Even so, don't jump to hard and fast conclusions. The other half of the living, dynamic structure of your memories must still be added to the mix. Now you need to examine how outwardly directed movement fits into the picture.

THE PRINCIPLE OF OUTWARDLY DIRECTED MOVEMENT IN MEMORIES

This aspect of childhood memories is a key indicator of our vitality. While core nuclear relationships address the internal emotional world and the need for security, movement addresses the need for growth and expansion and provides information on the individual's inclination to explore the outside world. (Remember that I am using "movement" as shorthand for the principle of outwardly directed movement.) But even if all human beings have a fundamental need for both security and growth, they don't all experience the same needs in the same way under the same circumstances and to the same degree. That's why I created four classifications: literal movement, symbolic movement, blocked movement and absence of movement. Furthermore, as we will see in a moment, this classification avoids rigid distinctions between the two dimensions of nuclearity and movement within your childhood memories.

Movement Expressed in Literal Terms

Let's review your three memories again and try to draw out the elements of movement in them. I expect you will find at least one. My experience suggests that two out of three people will find a visible expression of movement in their three memories. Are you one of those people? Can you identify a reference in your memories to a form of transportation (car, train, airplane or boat)? Or is the reference to a trip, vacation, hike, sports or another kind of recreation? If it does not appear in the first words you wrote, you will certainly find the movement-related expression in the details you added later, as I did in the case of my first memory. I first wrote, "I am in a garden that looks slightly neglected. I'm holding a brightly colored butterfly net and I'm trying to catch the butterflies flitting through the tall grass." I didn't add the following until later. "We are in the Vendée region of France, in my Uncle Jean and Aunt Jeanne's garden." If you do not find anything like that in your memories, movement may appear symbolically. Let's take a closer look.

Movement Expressed Symbolically

If you are patient and observant, your inner sleuth will enjoy tracking down symbolic movement in your memories. For example, it could appear as an individual activity (bike riding, roller skating) or a group game (hide-and-seek, cops and robbers or blind man's bluff). If that doesn't click, perhaps it's expressed in your doll buggy, your little sister's stroller, a model train or the little cars you liked to play with on the rug. Nothing there, either? Don't give up. What about the adults who appear in your three memories? What kind of work did they do? Did the group include a traveling salesman, a travel agent, taxi driver, history or geography teacher? (After all, history involves time travel and geography takes us through space.) If you're still not making any progress, perhaps there is a link to an internal voyage or a dream.

Is there a story of a flying carpet or a handsome prince on a white stallion who's come to ask your father for your hand? Look closely at the words you wrote. By reading between the lines, you should be able find some signs.

When Movement Is Blocked in Memories

Some people are active and determined regardless of circumstances, but they are not the majority. Few of us have such stable lives and unchanging natures. We struggle with inconsistent, if not contradictory, internal tensions. Do you remember Bertrand, the radiant young man with the painful, inexplicable sense that something was blocking his life? From that perspective, memories of movement that include a transition space between inside and outside (a garden, patio, balcony or cul-de-sac) are interesting because they reveal the psyche's remarkable sensitivity and ability to make distinctions as it tempers our perception of life and its uncertainties. Functioning simultaneously as a gas pedal ("Explore the outside world . . .") and a brake (". . . but stay inside these boundaries"), they represent an intermediate phase—let's call it a training ground—between the family and the larger world. Outwardly directed movement combined with classic core nuclearity offers a portrait of a traditional authoritarian, even repressive upbringing. (Children are children and must remain so, under the parents' authority.) Given that boys and girls are still raised differently, whether it's a matter of curfews, dating, clothing or household chores, these transition spaces figure more prominently in girls' memories than in boys.' They appear in boys' memories when they grew up with a strong parental authority.

When Movement Does Not Appear in Memories

As I said, analysis rarely fails to reveal a single element of movement in a series of three memories. Do you remember Marie-Claire, the young woman from Reunion Island whose three memories were all set within the confines of the house? If you do not find movement in any of your memories, remember that it can also be conspicuous by its absence. For example, "We never went out," "We had to stay in the house" and "I would have liked to learn to ride horseback, but my parents would never have allowed it."

We cannot possibly anticipate all the ways in which the human brain might express or code the notion of movement in a childhood memory because they are nearly infinite. I offer examples and possible paths just to give you a sense of the remarkable diversity of elements that relate, in varying degrees, to the principle of movement. It's your job to identify how your unconscious may have coded them and examine why it expressed them in a particular way or, on the contrary, chose to hold them back.

WHEN THE NUCLEARITY AND MOVEMENT PRINCIPLES MEET IN MEMORIES

Nuclearity represents verticality. In memories, it corresponds to generational, transgenerational and interpersonal relationships (including grandparents, parents, siblings and children) and has a temporal function. Movement represents horizontality because it indicates how we explore the world through our life experiences and has a spatial function. Humans move and develop within these two universal givens of time and space. Every three-memory series includes these dimensions of *verticality-time* ("Who am I, intrinsically, within my family, within the society?") and *horizontality-space* ("What is my world? How do I live in relation to my perceptions, understanding and conception of the world around me?").

If you cross-reference the *verticality-time-nuclearity* and *horizontality-space-movement* information, you will have two practical indicators that help you grasp both the living, dynamic structure and deeper meaning of your childhood memories. At the same time, this will help you understand how your childhood memories can have new relevance to your life today. Actually, "new" is not the right word. Memories do not "become relevant again." Their relevance evolves continuously because human life is not compartmentalized but is a living continuity. This is easy to understand. We don't go to sleep as children one night, wake up as adolescents the next morning and as adults the morning after. Rather, every life experience contributes to assembling the whole over time, just as every puzzle piece has a place in the whole.

You now have the tools to analyze your three memories correctly and should be able to use them together effectively. Take another look at the three childhood memories you wrote down. For the last time, ask yourself the following questions and try to answer them spontaneously.

- Is the general mood playful, serious, preachy, painful or neutral?

- Does the nuclearity principle appear in classic form, nonclassic form or not at all? (Please remember that whether your memories meet a particular standard is not a measure of "normalcy.")

- Do your memories deal primarily or exclusively with your relationship with your mother, your father, with the years you lived in, say, Chicago or Phoenix, your parochial school experience or your first house? Why is your mother (or your father, brother, sister) absent from your three memories? Does this reveal something? Based on that observation, can you find a connection between what the memories tell you about your childhood and your life today? Do your memories provide information on your self-image as a woman or a man?

- What is the setting for the events featured in your memories? Did the events occur during a vacation? Do they involve an accident, violence, aggression, illness or death? Is there a connection between these past events and how you view life today?

- With respect to the movement principle, do your memories indicate whether you have a stronger or a weaker tendency toward action? Do they suggest anything that might block your drive?

Make a note of all the images that come to mind and the words they suggest to you. Connect them and try to find a common denominator. That theme will provide information on your style of life and your attitude toward yourself, life and others.

In your memories, *nuclearity* represents the boat and *movement,* the rudder. The latter determines the direction, establishes the rhythm and supports the dynamic pace of your life. Your childhood memories will give you an idea of your tendencies, but we're talking about a compass, not a GPS system. Instead of trying to pin down, evaluate. Your childhood memories are not there to tell you what you know, but what you don't. This method will not help you determine whether you are an active, reactive or passive person, socially active or agoraphobic, stingy or generous. You probably know that already, better than anyone. Rather, my method for analyzing memories can provide information about experiences that you do not understand and help you address them. It is useful in dealing with situations that elude you or ones that you can't turn to your best advantage because you do not understand the underlying reasons. Perhaps these situations involve a pattern of failure or unexplained blockages, a history of disappointed expectations, stubbornness, resistance to change, an inability to think ahead or traps that you regularly set for yourself. If you know how to listen to your childhood memories, they will help you gain insight.

CHAPTER 14

Pulling Back
a Curtain

To see beauty that is too commonplace
to capture others' imagination.
—AUGUSTE RODIN[1]

THE UNCONSCIOUS IS AN EFFECTIVE MANAGER

Our conscious and unconscious are always at work on our perceptions and our assessment of them. The conscious says, "I am experiencing such-and-such an event. What does it inspire in me? Have I already been through this? Will this event or action make me feel secure or at risk? Can I connect it to another experience I am familiar with, have lived through, suffered or addressed?" Our unconscious speaks its own language. "You are experiencing such-and-such an event, but how does it weigh in the current context? Will it change the overall balance? Should I connect this event to others that you have already experienced, evaluated, arranged and recorded in memory? Should I let this information enter, censor it or hold back just a part of it? Is the self capable of handling the confrontation between two pieces of conflicting information? Is it strong enough for that?" As you can see, the unconscious may censor, but it also protects.

Nothing that is created, happens or is produced within us occurs by accident. Nothing is without purpose. In other words, everything—thoughts, spirit, perceptions, actions, dreams and even neuroses—has a meaning and a use. Even if the purpose is unknown to us, everything within us is intended to be adapted and choreographed to work together. The same is true for the way we remember things. Nothing that we remember or is remembered within us is random. I can still hear the philosopher Paul Ricoeur explain in his interview on French television, "We say to ourselves, 'Do you remember?' 'Of course!' And suddenly fragments of the past are recalled. This means that forgetting is also a forgetting kept in reserve, a forgetting that protects against itself, against its own erasing."

The unconscious is a prudent banker. It doesn't let just anyone into the safe deposit box of our memories at any moment and it doesn't mix stocks, securities and liquid assets. It manages our memories wisely, protecting us from others and ourselves, for example, by causing us to bury or forget certain unpleasant or painful memories or to mourn a disillusionment or a betrayal. It can also adapt to every new circumstance and, in·particular, the changes within us. For example, it can allow memories to resurface when we are strong and prepared to handle the incredible emotion (Freud called it the "disturbing strangeness") that is connected to memories and can have a destructive impact.[2]

Our unconscious does not react to "headline news events," but it does operate an efficient search and retrieval system. It seeks out the sensitive memories and perceptions it knows we are capable of confronting and allows them to return to the surface. What's more, it can even release new memories and the new feelings linked to them. Psychotherapists are very familiar with this phenomenon. They often hear people say, "Wow, all of a sudden I remember" or "That's odd, I had never thought of that." These little gifts from the unconscious reward us for the hard work involved in the effort to understand. But in the broader sense, it's larger than that. It's as if a curtain were pulled back, revealing (or re-revealing) chapters of your life.

MEMORIES ARE THE MARKERS OF OUR DEEPEST SELF

While I was writing this book, entire memories would come back to me, often at the most unexpected moments. I remembered that when I was a child, I used to love playing marbles with my friends on the playground. We would set up a toy soldier or cowboy and try to hit the figure with a marble from ten or twelve feet away. If the marble knocked the soldier down, the player won. The winner got to keep all the marbles that missed. I was crazy about this game. When it was time to go back to class, I could think about only one thing: playing again at the next recess. But when I analyze that memory today, I see that what mattered to me was the sense of victory and power, not the marbles and the soldiers. I also realize that these victories can be lonely because wanting to win at any cost isolates you a bit from other people.

Memories can provide insight into a state of mind you didn't completely understand at the time. The desire to win at any cost was a constant feature of my childhood, as was creating relationships based on competition. That makes sense because as the youngest of four, I had to push harder to keep up. What strikes me today is the feeling of solitude superimposed on my victories. I never understood that before. Isolation is inevitable because winning requires a huge personal investment and the temporary sidelining of the self. This characterizes all the battles I have fought in my life. From now on, I will pay particular attention to this issue and make a special effort to draw close to my friends.

And what about you? Do certain emotions rise to the surface as you read these pages? This book is not neutral. Stirring up memories necessarily draws you in. Perhaps you cursed me for causing disagreeable, unhappy or even terrible memories to reappear, but perhaps the process also brought back a tender childhood memory and moved you more than you expected.

These tools for understanding and interpreting memories are powerful. You may need to return to a particular issue or situation linked to one of your memories and think about it further. Perhaps you were not careful enough when you wrote it down, did not immediately recognize its relevance or just didn't feel especially involved. That doesn't matter. As you re-read the chapters that interest you, you will quickly be able to evaluate your memories because the guidelines for interpretation introduced here apply widely, even universally.

MEMORIES OFFER A REMARKABLE TOOL FOR SELF-KNOWLEDGE AND SELF-TRANSCENDENCE

I have long wondered why we ascribe so little significance to memories. Is it because they emanate from our conscious life? If anyone can call up any memory at any moment, what's the attraction, the mystery, the appeal? After all, nothing is more ordinary than a memory. Amnesiacs aside, everyone has memories and talks about them. And we all know that the rarer the object, the greater its value. Dreams have higher status because they can veil themselves in mystery. Even if they are trivial or obscene, they maintain a certain aura of respectability because they come to us pure, as a product of the unconscious, and their hazy outlines elude us. We have learned to accept the notion that, "If it's my unconscious speaking, what can I do about it?" Having an obscene dream is one thing. Remembering an obscene act you performed is quite another. The first leaves us perplexed, while the second leaves us feeling guilty. What's more, if that obscene act conflicts with our moral principles, our unconscious will know how to put things in order and will lead us to censor, repress or forget it.

Our memories are not the poor relations of our inner life. It's time to abandon that prejudice. They have their complexity, language, latent content, hidden meaning and forms of expression too. They are an unparalleled source of information about how we perceive life, other people and the world. They also help us understand the particular way in which we face or avoid difficult life situations, manifest our resistance and follow the paths that life presents and sometimes forces us to take.

The analysis of childhood memories is not an obscure decoding of past events but a tool for self-knowledge and, as such, for self-evaluation and self-transcendence.

- Analyzing our memories allows us to shake off timeworn myths about ourselves that are based on fragmented, narrow, awkward and often negative clichés that have little to do with the complex richness of who we really are. Those myths are expressed when someone says, "I know myself very well." That's normal. Our culture, environment and upbringing have shaped that image and it's only logical that we would try to match our reflection to it. However, we are left with only a vague and misleading sense of ourselves. By analyzing our memories, we can move beyond appearances, find our true selves and be enriched by incorporating the new images those memories reveal.

- Analyzing our memories allows us to deepen our sense of ourselves. They permit us to take a certain distance from and offer a more detached view of situations we have experienced or been subjected to. They help us draw a more accurate picture of ourselves, less marked by the stamp of our personality and character. They guide us toward a new way of understanding ourselves.

Working to achieve self-knowledge is and always has been an invaluable undertaking. It is even more critical in this time of hypercommunication and the heightened presence of media in our lives. Self-knowledge is invaluable in every realm, whether professional, social or romantic. The person who lacks the minimum tools for achieving self-knowledge—someone who does not try to understand where he stands in relation to life, other people and the outside world—is quickly cast off, both literally and figuratively. Today, reflecting on who you are, assessing your life and its direction, and seeing your existence as a work in progress are as much a part of staying healthy as caring for your body. And you can't cut corners. That's particularly true for men. In the past, they could play the patriarchy card, but those days are over. Women's liberation paved the way and now men are invited to follow, whether they like it or not.

Self-knowledge is like a mountain with many slopes. Each route to the top is different. Interpreting childhood memories is the "royal road" to the summit. It may not be the easiest path, but it is one of the most productive. It may be demanding and require methodological and scientific rigor, but the rewards are more than equal to the climb.

Appendix
The Analysis of Childhood Memories in Psychotherapy

These things do I within, in that vast court of my memory....
There also meet I with myself, and recall myself... There be all
which I remember, either on my own experience or other's credit.
—AUGUSTINE, *CONFESSIONS*[1]

A WORLD OF VALUES

Before concluding, I would like to say a few words to health professionals (psychiatrists, psychologists, psychotherapists and psychiatric nurses) who deal with patients' childhood memories and would like to use my method for analyzing and interpreting them. I am thinking particularly of those who are new to the field. I will discuss my own professional experience as a psychoanalytic psychotherapist, with the understanding that each person will adapt what I say to his or her own practice.

When a person gathers up her courage and makes an appointment, it's generally because she is experiencing a major identity crisis or a problem she considers to be serious. People often delay the moment of decision for as long as possible and call only when their back is against the wall.

Our first task is to listen to what the individual brings to the therapist's office. The problems she describes will not necessarily be the ones that prompted her to make the call, but will likely be more general and less embarrassing to acknowledge. To paraphrase Freud, we would call them screen problems: a particular straw broke a particular camel's back. That straw usually—and paradoxically—has nothing to do with the camel or its back. The camel is the psychological context, the multiplicity of problems in the person's life. The camel's back is the threshold of tolerance, the limits to or degree of stress the person can endure. The straw could be an appointment that someone failed to keep, an unjustified scolding or yet another disillusionment, insult or betrayal.

After I've given the individual time to express what is on her mind and as I begin to have a sense of the problem, I ask what she expects of me. In a way, this anticipates the initial tacit contract between us. "I'm here because I don't know what I'm doing anymore," "I want you to help me understand what is happening to me," "I absolutely have to save this relationship," "I'm so unhappy and I can't figure things out by myself at this point," or "A question? I don't have a question." The decision to start therapy always implies a question, but the patient does not always know what it is. French psychoanalyst Jacques Lacan understood that when he said, "They do not know that they know," so we must accept this interim state of affairs. If, during the first session, we can create a semblance of order out of everything the patient says, we will have made considerable headway.

If the individual does arrive with a specific question, I will naturally direct the session toward that topic. At the same time, I make sure not to rush there. In psychotherapy, you have to listen to everything, even (and perhaps especially) what is unsaid.

If I sense that the process lacks focus and direction, is paradoxical or contradictory, or that the individual is trying to control the session, I may choose to change the rhythm by asking her to tell me a few early childhood memories, and even several more. As I mentioned earlier, the response to that request provides valuable information that may be even more valuable than what was provided earlier in the session. It offers a different approach to developing the case history. At that key moment, the therapist still carries some weight in the exchange. Within a few moments or at the next session, the individual may lead us where she wants to go. The patient will almost always gain the upper hand in the verbal sparring. She knows what her problem is and has already explored the hidden recesses of her resistance, sometimes over a period of years. As the sessions continue, the therapist may regain some ground but will have lost time. In the worst case, the patient gains the upper hand in the relationship, which makes the ongoing psychotherapy much more difficult.

Ready access to three or four childhood memories provides a fresh body of material, unmarked by the transference and counter-transference that is part of every consultation. They provide me a springboard or an additional jumping-off place if the sessions break down or get stuck. They also constitute a baseline I can use to remind myself of a particular aspect of the individual's core issue or evaluate her progress and remind her, with proof at hand, how the problem was framed initially. Childhood memories indicate a state of mind at a particular moment. Is that state of mind the same? Has it changed? Has the nature of her present problems changed?

EXPLORING PERSONALITY

Childhood memories can provide information that may be new and unexpected to the patient. As the therapist collects those memories, carefully and consciously, he or she must assess what the person sitting in the other chair is capable of hearing about herself and what may be impossible to accept for the moment. If, for example, childhood memories reveal a problem that existed with the father (or mother, sister or brother), but the two get along quite well today, it could be inappropriate or awkward to disclose that "raw" information.

When I analyze memories using my method, I always take some time afterward to explain the meaning of my process. I discuss the living, dynamic structure of memories and the unexpected opportunities for insight they offer. Without going into too much detail, I explain the principles of nuclearity and outwardly directed movement and I spend a little time on the presence or absence of nuclearity in memories.

It is important to find the right tone and manner when presenting the issue of analysis and interpretation. I propose a method for exploring personality that incorporates childhood memories, not a lie detector test or a method for revealing some shameful neurosis. The most important point is to use the information that emerges from the analysis of memories to identify the constructive aspects of the individual's problem or crisis. We know that reassurance is critical in therapy, particularly during the early sessions, even if the placebo effect plays a role.

The difficult or sensitive points that the analysis of memories reveals are not intended to devastate the patient or undermine her morale. Quite the contrary—the interesting and useful images we can highlight offer very concrete lessons.

Analyzing and interpreting childhood memories reveals character traits, temperaments, attitudes, behaviors, problems, inabilities and feelings of failure that the individual may sense strongly but wants to hide. When the analysis reveals such traits or behaviors, if the patient does not already understand the theoretical framework, she might see the process as a game of three-card monte rather than a legitimate psychological undertaking.[2] We must always be transparent and explain the approach so that the patient knows that this involves analysis, not fortune-telling. If a memory does not speak to me, I tell the patient because I know she will not hold it against me.

ANTICIPATING OR CONFIRMING THE CASE HISTORY

I may move into the analysis of three childhood memories either to move the case history process forward or to confirm it.

- Anticipation: I turn to memory analysis if the patient is trying to control me or is overly resistant, or if I sense that my own attitude may be too subjective or projective if, for example, the patient is a well-known individual, receives a lot of media attention or is part of that person's inner circle (for example, the son of a politician or the wife of a widely recognized scientist).

In such a situation, childhood memories provide material for analysis before the "official story" masks the sensitive reality of the patient's malaise.

When the content of the communication and the interpersonal exchange are already rich, and the analysis of the three memories would not add to but might detract from the quality of the conversation, I do not rely on the analysis of memories. We always rigidify the process when we try to force it to follow a particular scheme. I work in the moment, assessing whether to direct the conversation toward the analysis of the memories or allow the session to take its own course.

- Confirmation: An experienced psychotherapist does not need a specific method to detect the pathology he or she is dealing with (from hysteria to obsession, paranoia, schizophrenia, depression, borderline personality disorder or dependency). Over the course of the session, the subject's personality, character and behavior generally speak for themselves.

Analysis of the three childhood memories often proves useful in confirming or invalidating what emerges from the case history process or my intuition. It is convenient, does not take a lot of time and offers an additional valuable tool for gaining insight.

When analyzing and interpreting childhood memories, a professional must always be prepared to challenge the framework in the face of an unexpected piece of information. I advise against forcing the facts at hand to fit the interpretation. Imagine you are driving down the highway and try to pass another car. If something unexpected happens just as you are passing, you must slow immediately, return to your lane and wait for the next opportunity to pull out safely.

This method of analyzing and interpreting childhood memories moves the process forward and acts as a quality control. First, it provides a quick scan of the individual's psychological tendencies and screens for the difficulties and inherent restrictions she faces in life. It also highlights symptomology and neurotic tendencies that may emerge, although they may be established in other ways.

It is an effective social barometer to the extent that it provides information on the individual's childhood relationship patterns (nuclearity) and how she may have compensated when they proved difficult, inappropriate, inadequate or intolerable. Childhood memories thus offer a wealth of information on the individual's openness toward others and the world.

We can also learn about the individual's relationships with her partner, family members and close friends, as well as how she views her relationship with the larger world. When we cross-reference information related to the nuclearity principle with information related to the outwardly directed movement principle, the individual's behavioral tendencies emerge, from her stance toward life (cautious or courageous) to how she positions herself with respect to others and her ability to act or react. The curve of the individual's emotional maturity emerges as we observe the process.

Because memories evolve based on the individual's current situation, as Alfred Adler noted, I find it useful to revisit the three childhood memories from time to time, or even request three new ones, as a way to monitor the individual's development since the start of therapy. Without turning this into a systematic or statistical assessment, I can observe her development as both agent and subject of change. Having memorized or taken notes on the three childhood memories at the beginning of therapy, when necessary I can show her what the memories she recounted at the start told us and review her development since then. If the person is experiencing a regressive phase, the analysis and interpretation of three new childhood memories will indicate the area of life in which this regression is occurring. In such cases, I will usually look to information drawn from the movement principle (as you recall, nuclearity = security; movement = expansion).

AGE RANGES AND
SENSE OF HISTORICAL CONTINUITY

I should mention the age ranges into which the three memories fall because they provide interesting information, if only about the individual's sense of historicity. As noted earlier, I use that term to describe how we integrate the continuum of our past, present and future into our present life.

We must distinguish between what these categories mean in and of themselves (they only state the obvious) and what useful information they may reveal, in phenomenological terms, about the individual's basic issue. Obviously the nuclearity principle will leave a stronger mark on very early childhood memories (from around the age of one or two) than the movement principle, since at that age a child is more likely to be nursing than setting off to conquer distant lands.

However, it would be very interesting to observe the setting of the memory, the people who appear and the events or actions featured. If someone tells me, "When I was about a year old, I went to my grandmother's house because my mother was going to have a baby. I remember being very scared because I was afraid that I would never see her again," the elements could help us gain an overall understanding of the individual. My friend Jody described having her picture taken at a photographer's studio when she was around eighteen months old. She remembered that the photographer clowned behind the camera to make her smile. She didn't think he was funny and recalled saying to herself, "What's the matter with him? Why is he pretending to be so stupid? He's acting like an idiot!" Would a child that age have that kind of vocabulary? It doesn't really matter. Even if she used her own form of speech, what counts is the particular memory she retained.

In general, the four- to six-year age range is the richest period for childhood memories. As Jody's memory shows, some childhood memories reach even further back. Although some may be challenged as secondhand recollections (based on stories told by parents or other family members), others may have been stored from a very young age. Likewise, people sometimes tell psychotherapists that they have no powerful memories from before the age of ten or eleven. This may involve resistance if the person does not want to remember, or even self-denial or a way to discredit oneself ("I am so insignificant that I don't have anything to tell you"). However, some people unconsciously create amnesia to close off a part of their childhood. We must look to the person's overall psychology for the reasons underlying this remarkable form of forgetting (for example, what purpose is served by remembering nothing?). As I have said elsewhere, whatever the explanation (including trauma, family distress, changed family situation or early loss of a loved one), I try to be very gentle and careful as the individual slowly returns to full awareness after experiencing a reduced level of emotional consciousness.

- When childhood memories date back to the age of one, I believe that reflects an exceptional memory system. While we may find this an impressive feat, such memories should be treated very cautiously. They almost always refer to the mother—that first, important Other—and the dyadic relationship she establishes with her baby. As you might expect, information regarding that very early period will necessarily emphasize the emotional. I call these "cartilage memories" because of their fragile nature. The key material available for analysis is linked to security and emotion, often reflecting the oral stage. Given that these memories refer back practically to infancy, this seems natural.

- Childhood memories from one to three years of age express a strong sense of historicity and also indicate a secure, receptive parental and familial environment. Core nuclear relationships will play a key role here, revealing how and to what extent the child has invested in the relationship with the mother, father and siblings and, later, the rest of the family. Movement will be present, but to a lesser extent because with a few exceptions, the child still lives in the nest, with minimal exposure to the outside world. These memories will include statements like, "When my father came home," or "I looked out the window at the cars driving by."

- When memories refer to the period between three and six years of age, I assume that they play a normal role in the individual's life. We can expect the nuclearity and movement principles to be well balanced. The child's social experiences are expanding at this age. Spaces like a garden or courtyard—mediators between the inside and outside worlds—will continue to play an important role, but the external world is starting to take shape. The nursery school or day care center lays the path outward.

- People often recount memories from the period between six and twelve years of age. These memories reveal more about anecdote, action or mood than emotional context. After a certain age, elements of movement predominate over those relating to nuclearity.

APPLYING THIS METHOD

This method is suited to many areas of psychology and psychotherapy and to all approaches (individual, analytic, behavioral, family and systems therapy). Practitioners should assess their patient population, determine when it would be appropriate to use this three-memory method and evaluate its purpose and relevance. Regardless of the patient's age (child, young adult, mature adult or elderly), the full spectrum of the nuclearity and displacement dimensions should be present.

Professionals in the child protection and abuse prevention fields may find this to be an excellent way to establish an active dialogue with children and adolescents, particularly in cases of early childhood trauma. My method for analyzing and interpreting childhood memories will be extremely useful at the start of child therapy (although not before the second or even third session) because, in general, children's memories directly reflect their current experience. It may seem odd to ask a child of eight or ten for childhood memories, but when a child trusts her therapist, she will speak simply and openly. Add a touch of humor and she will be cooperative and curious.

Last, incorporating my method of analyzing and interpreting three memories in other approaches or personality tests may prove useful in assessments (including psychological and skills assessment) because it provides specific information on the individual's social interactions and behaviors. However, this process must include privacy protections because it quickly enters personal and intimate spheres that extend beyond personality mapping.

A SCIENCE OF MEMORIES

The framework of my method can be applied to anyone, regardless of origin. Just as all humans breathe, eat, drink, sleep and dream, they all think about, refer to or forget memories. Whatever an individual's geographic or cultural origin, the living, dynamic structure of his or her memories will include nuclearity and outward-directed movement, even when those memories reflect religious tradition or are obscured by folk wisdom or superstition.

Every human being has parents or adults who play that role, whether adoptive parents, older brothers or sisters, guardians or others. Every human being lives within a family constellation and social network that reflect varying degrees of structure. All have experienced problems in relationships with these key individuals (nuclearity) and have discovered and come face-to-face with the outside world (movement).

Classic nuclearity will likely predominate among individuals from strongly patriarchal societies (like the Middle East) and those who practice ancestor worship (Asian and Indian cultures), compared to individuals from Western cultures. On the other hand, it would be logical to assume that movement would play a particular role among nomadic cultures, for example. However, setting aside these differences (which can be controlled for easily), nothing would exclude the interplay of the nuclearity and movement principles.

This book offers an analytic and interpretive method based on three childhood memories. The tools proposed are based on a solid foundation, not conjecture or speculation. Alfred Adler said there are no "chance" memories. Similarly, coincidence and fantasy have no place in their interpretation. Insofar as the nuclearity and movement principles provide a verifiable reference system that permits the practitioner to correlate the information received, we can describe this method as scientific, just as we refer to a science of dreams (to which I subscribe, in general terms).

This book presents the current state of my work and observations. It is an introduction, not a result. I would be delighted to see individuals working in areas that may rely on this method continue the research initiated in this work. The way is open.

Notes

Foreword

1. Patrick Estrade, *Comment je me suis débarrassé de moi-même: Les sept portes du changement* (Paris: Robert Laffont, 2004).

Chapter 1

1. "I would never investigate a personality without asking for the first memory." Alfred Adler, *What Life Could Mean to You*, trans. Colin Brett (Oxford: One World, 1992), 72.

2. "According to this technique, we must not attach particular importance to any of what we hear and should lend the same 'free-floating' attention to everything." Sigmund Freud, *La technique psychanalytique* (Paris: PUF, 1953), 63.

3. Recall Wilhelm Dilthey's famous comment seeking to distinguish between the natural sciences and the "spiritual" sciences: "Nature we explain, but the life of the soul we must understand." Wilhelm Dilthey, *Introduction to the Human Sciences,* ed. Ramón Betanzos (Detroit: Wayne State University Press, 1988); Dilthey, *Introduction à l'étude des sciences humaines* (Paris: PUF, 1942), 154.

4. Friedrich Nietzsche, *Daybreak: Thoughts on the Prejudices of Morality,* ed. Maudemarie Clark and Brian Leitner (Cambridge: Cambridge University Press, 1982), 34.

5. Henri Bergson, *L'Énergie spirituelle* (Paris: PUF, 1919), 52, 57.

6. Quoted by Ludwig Binswanger, *Introduction à l'analyse existentielle* (Paris: Minuit, 1971), 61.

7. In 2004 Philippe Villemus published a hodgepodge entitled *J'ai oublié* (I Forgot). The collection of forgotten memories starts with "I have forgotten the brand of spiked soccer shoes that my mother bought me with money she'd saved up for weeks" and ends, at the 445th, with "I have forgotten all my dreams from childhood, but not all the ones from adolescence."

8. Carl Gustav Jung, "The Personal and Collective Unconscious," in *The Collected Works of C.G. Jung,* ed. H. Read, M. Fordham, G. Adler, and Wm. McGuire, Bollingen Series 20 (Princeton: Princeton University Press, 1953–1979), para. 103. Cited at www.psychceu.com/Jung/sharplexicon.html.

9. Carl Gustav Jung, *Psychologie de l'inconscient* (Geneva: Librairie de l'Université/Georg & Cie, 1978), 123.

10. Friedrich Nietzsche, *Beyond Good and Evil* (Amherst, N.Y.: Prometheus, 1989), 86.

CHAPTER 2

1. "During the epoch which may be described as prescientific, men had no difficulty in finding an explanation of dreams. When they remembered a dream after waking up, they regarded it as either a favorable or hostile manifestation by higher powers, demonic and divine." Sigmund Freud, *On Dreams, The Standard Edition* (New York: Norton, 1965), 5.

2. Freud, *On Dreams*, p. 37. I also found a comprehensive bibliography on dreams in an excerpt of a book published on the Internet, *Histoire des recherches sur le rêve: Un inédit de 1801 fait la jonction entre la conception ancienne et moderne du rêve,* by Yehoshua Rahamim Dufour, www.modia.org/publications/desjardins.html.

3. Stefan Zweig, *Freud* (Paris: Stock, Stock Plus, 1978), 100.

4. Sigmund Freud, *Psychopathology of Everyday Life* (New York: Norton, 1965), 43.

5. Adler, *What Life Could Mean to You*, 87.

6. Adler, *What Life Could Mean to You*, 90.

7. Adler, *What Life Could Mean to You*, 92.

8. Jean-Yves and Marc Tadié, *Le sens de la mémoire* (Paris: Gallimard/Folio, 1999), 204.

9. Sigmund Freud, *Essais de psychanalyse* (Paris: Payot, 1975).

10. Adler, *What Life Could Mean to You,* 72.

11. I think this is what led the translator and commentator of the French edition of *What Life Could Mean to You* to add the following footnote. "The remarkable ease with which Alfred Adler seems to be able to perceive intuitively is the result not of the sweeping application of a rigid approach, but of clinical experience acquired over many years. It allowed him to set out the general framework of the case and insert each detail whose meaning appeared consistent with the context. In this method . . . details acquire reliable value only when compared to all other features."

12. I analyzed this question in depth in my book *Parents/enfants: Pourquoi ça bloque?* (Saint-Jean-de-Braye: Dangles, 1996).

13. The National Association for Self-Esteem is based in Fulton, Maryland, and its Web site is at www.self-esteem-nase.org.

CHAPTER 3

1. Freud, *Psychopathology of Everyday Life,* 135.

2. Carolyn Rovee-Collier and Scott Adler, "La recherche," *La mémoire* 267 (1994): 740.

3. Edouard Zarifian, "Alzheimer: Cerveau sans mémoire," *La recherche,* January 2003.

4. See the *New York Times* Web page: http://query.nytimes.com/gst/fullpage.html?sec =health&res=9B05E4D6163FF933A05753C1A96E958260.

5. Tadié, *Le sens de la mémoire*, 308.

6. Freud, *Psychopathology of Everyday Life,* 135.

7. In its June 2005 report, *ATD Quart Monde* noted that life expectancy in France is 83.8 years for women and 76.7 years for men. The University of California's *Wellness Letter,*

April 2007, reports that in the United States in 2004, life expectancy for females at birth was 80.4 years and for males, 75.2 years.

8. For information on memory skills research and activities, see soundmedicine.iu .edu/segment.php4?seg=1059.

9. New indications for the brain-related use of omega–3s continue to emerge, including memory, attention deficit disorders, hyperactivity, bipolar disorder, dementia and Alzheimer's disease.

10. David Servan-Schreiber, *The Instinct to Heal* (Emmaus, Pa.: Rodale, 2004), 132.

11. Freud, *Psychopathology of Everyday Life,* chaps. 1–4.

12. Cited at www.tregouet.org/article.php3?id_article=149#sommaire,_31.

13. Patrick Estrade, *Comment je me suis débarrassé de moi-même* (Paris: Robert Laffont, 2004).

14. Freud, *Psychopathology of Everyday Life,* 46.

15. Freud, *Psychopathology of Everyday Life*, 47–48.

16. Cited at www.tregouet.org/article.php3?id_article=388.

17. Antoine Guédeney, "Donner du sens à une expérience insensée," in *Ces enfants qui tiennent le coup* (Revigny-sur-Ornain: Hommes et Perspectives, 1998), 22–23.

18. Paul Ricoeur, interview by Jean Blain, www.lire.fr/entretien.asp?idC=36471&idTC =4&idR=201&idG.

19. The word "dialectic" should be understood in its contemporary meaning. My philosophy minidictionary, *Les termes philosophiques* (Paris: Marabout, 1990), notes, "The term 'dialectic' refers to systems of thought in which several elements are in relationship to each other."

CHAPTER 4

1. Carl Gustav Jung, *L'Âme et la vie* (Paris: Buchet/Chastel, 1963), 333.

2. Antoine de Saint-Exupéry, *The Little Prince,* trans. Katherine Woods (New York: Harcourt, Brace & World, 1943), 70.

3. In psychology, we refer to a two-person relationship as a dyad. When I spoke of a triad above, I was referring to the mother-father-child relationship.

4. Dominique Simonnet, *Vivent les bébés! Ce que savent les petits d'homme* (Paris: Le Seuil, 1983), 54.

5. Didier Dumas, *Et l'enfant créa le père* (Paris: Hachette littérature, 2000), 18.

6. Christiane Olivier, *Les enfants de Jocaste: L'empreinte de la mère* (Paris: Denoël, 2001), 177.

7. Juan David Nasio, "L'Oedipe: un mythe indispensable," *Journal des psychologues,* September 1994, 81.

8. Nasio, "L'Oedipe," 81.

9. Nasio, "L'Oedipe," 81.

10. This choice of words is not completely correct because grandparents are usually considered to be part of the extended family. In *Le dictionnaire des thérapies familiales:*

Théories et pratiques (Paris: Payot, 1987), Jacques Miermont writes, "The extended family refers to family members like grandparents, uncles, aunts, nephews, etc." I distinguish between them because grandparents play a particular role in childhood memories, which is not systematically the case for the rest of the extended family.

11. This is why we should not compare memories of events experienced with grandparents to those with parents because they differ in their very nature. The first are governed by the pleasure principle, while the latter reflect the reality principle.

CHAPTER 5

1. This is similar to the feeling reported by people who are beginning psychotherapy. Being the center of attention and the focus of the conversation is not easy. We're afraid of exaggerating, expressing opinions that might be too categorical, saying too much and being a tattletale. But at the same time, it's a wonderful opportunity to talk about yourself to someone who will listen to and understand you.

2. Medical imaging shows that two different regions of the brain are activated.

CHAPTER 6

1. The October 2006 thirtieth anniversary issue of *Psychologie Heute* (a popular German psychology magazine for women) was devoted to memory and featured three articles on the subject. The reference here appears on page 23. The editors printed the cover on silver paper, which gave a mirror effect. Given the topic, I think that was a clever choice.

2. Jean-Pierre Changeux, *Neuronal Man: The Biology of Mind* (New York: Pantheon, 1985).

3. That reminds me of Bertrand Russell's comment, which I can't resist including. "A process which led from the amoeba to man appeared to philosophers to be obviously progress—though whether the amoeba would agree with this opinion is not known" (*A Free Man's Worship and Other Essays,* 1976), chap. 2. Cited by Alexander Mitscherlich in *Vers la société sans pères* (Paris: Gallimard, 1969).

4. Hugo Hamilton, *The Speckled People* (London: Fourth Estate, 2003), 201.

5. Alphonse de Lamartine, "Milly ou la terre natale," in *Les harmonies poétiques et religieuses* (Paris: Gallimard/La Pléiade, 1963).

CHAPTER 7

1. Abraham Maslow, *Toward a Psychology of Being* (Princeton, N.J.: Van Nostrand, 1968), 49.

2. The window is an interesting image in memories because it mediates between the internal and external worlds. It is a passageway for seeing and perceiving the safe, nourishing world that is the home and the external world to be explored. As an aside, when a woman complains that her husband does not help out with household tasks, I recommend that she assign him jobs that involve the external world rather than the internal, like cleaning the windows, doing errands or taking out the garbage, rather than dusting or washing floors. However, my recommendation does not always produce the desired effect.

3. Riding in an elevator can be a strange experience. The artificial proximity to others, the fact that we are at the mercy of some external mechanism and the potential for danger all lead us to behave in odd ways. One person checks her watch. Another pretends to rummage around in his pocket. A third seems fascinated by the passing of the floors. I would also like to set something straight. Some people say they are afraid of riding an elevator. Actually, they are not afraid of the trip up (the ascent). It's the fall (the descent) that makes them anxious.

4. Franz Kafka, "The Burrow," in *The Complete Stories* (New York: Schocken, 1971), 325.

5. I think this is what prompted educators to develop the first kindergartens, although "garden" was often a matter of name only. The key was to provide young children with a setting in which they could experience interpersonal and community relationships with other children their age.

6. Parents sometimes draw absurd conclusions. The answer given by David's father reminds me of a silly joke, but one that illustrates this reductive thinking. Every day, a man goes down to the train tracks carrying a flask and pours an unknown liquid onto the tracks. A neighbor observes this mysterious ceremony from his window. Finally, his curiosity gets the better of him. He goes downstairs and says to the man, "You know, I've been watching you for several days and I can't help but wonder what you're doing with that flask." "It's simple," the other man says. "The liquid I pour on the tracks keeps elephants away." The neighbor says, "You know, I've lived here for a long time and I've never seen an elephant in the area." "You see," the other man says, "it's working!"

7. Scientists working on the U.S. spacecraft launched in 1977 made a clever choice when they named the probe *Voyager.* The goal was not simply to send it into space, but to gather data and send back images, which it continues to do.

Chapter 8

1. This recalls the famous exchange in Molière's play, *The Bourgeois Gentleman.* "Well, your first choice could be to put it just the way you've said it: 'Fair Marquise, your lovely eyes make me die of love,' or then you might say, 'Of love, fair Marquise, your lovely eyes make me die,' Or else: 'Of lovely love, your eyes, Marquise fair, make me die.' Or then: 'Your lovely eyes, fair Marquise, die of love; make me.' Or yet again: 'Make me die of love, lovely eyes, your fair Marquise.'" http://moliere-in-english.com/bourgeois.html.

2. By "sublimate" I mean to divert or turn a desire toward a socially acceptable object.

3. Sigmund Freud, *The Interpretation of Dreams,* trans. A. A. Brill (New York: Macmillan, 1913), preface to the first edition.

Chapter 9

1. Anne Ancelin-Schützenberger, *Aïe, mes aïeux!* (Paris: Desclée de Brouwer, 1993); Ancelin-Schützenberger, *The Ancestor Syndrome: Transgenerational Psychotherapy and the Hidden Links in the Family Tree* (London: Routledge, 1998).

2. Ancelin-Schützenberger, *Aïe, mes aïeux,* 21.

3. Ancelin-Schützenberger, *Aïe, mes aïeux,* 59–60.

4. See the excellent book on this subject by Elizabeth Loftus and Katherine Ketchum, *The Myth of Repressed Memory* (New York: St. Martin's, 1994).

CHAPTER 10

1. Childhood trauma became a subject of serious interest only around twenty years ago. In an article about psychotraumatic disorders, psychiatrist Gérard Lopez explains, "The American Psychiatric Association only recognized post-traumatic stress disorder (PTSD) in the 1980s. Since that time, PTSD has become the most commonly diagnosed psychiatric disorder among children who have experienced a traumatic event." "Progrès en pédiatrie," in *Pédiatrie sociale* (Rueil-Malmaison: Doin Éditeurs, 2004), 265.

2. Susan Forward, *Toxic Parents: Overcoming Their Hurtful Legacy and Reclaiming Your Life* (New York: Bantam, 1989).

3. Similarly, I have created a blog as a sanctuary for memories where people can relieve themselves of painful or haunting childhood memories by sharing them with others. The process is anonymous. For the URL, see the resources section at the end of the book.

4. Marcel Rufo, *Œdipe toi-même* (Paris: Le Livre de poche, 2002).

5. Quoted in Guénard, *Tagueurs d'espérance,* 12.

6. Quoted by Anne Ancelin-Schützenberger, *Aïe, mes aïeux,* 112.

7. The uneven impact of trauma suggests that history may not be destiny. Boris Cyrulnik, *Un merveilleux malheur* (Paris: Odile Jacob, 1996), 16.

8. forum.aufeminin.com/forum/psych01/f44364_psych[COND]0[COND]1-souvenirs-ecrans.html.

9. Patrick Estrade, "Pédophilie: Les murs du silence," *Féminin Psycho,* September-October-November, 110.

10. Alice Miller, *The Truth Will Set You Free: Overcoming Emotional Blindness and Finding Your True Adult Self* (New York: Basic, 2001). My views on "poisonous pedagogy" and the origins of violence tend to be close to Alice Miller's. I have developed some of my own ideas on this issue, which are discussed in my book, *Comment je me suis débarrassé de moi-même,* 174ff.

11. Estrade, *Comment je me suis débarrassé de moi-même,* 61.

12. Estrade, *Comment je me suis débarrassé de moi-même,* 117.

13. Estrade, *Comment je me suis débarrassé de moi-même,* 119.

14. "The final outcome of analysis is to release the patient, belatedly but definitively, from the obsessive fear of the trauma of birth, a fear that had never disappeared from his unconscious." Otto Rank, *Le traumatisme de la naissance* (Paris: Payot, 1976), 15.

CHAPTER 11

1. Hermann Hesse, *Siddhartha, Demian and Other Writings* (New York: Continuum, 1999), 113–114.

2. Carole Damiani, "La prise en charge des personnes traumatisées," *Culture en mouvement, Le débat,* March 2001.

3. Milan Kundera, *The Art of the Novel* (New York: Grove, 1986), 102–103.

CHAPTER 12

1. Michel Juffé, *Les fondements du lien social: Sociologie d'aujourd'hui* (Paris: PUF, 1995).

2. Patrick Estrade, *Un reflet d'infini* (Paris: Dervy, 2000).

CHAPTER 13

1. This may also correspond to a current conflict with a parent that is causing you to avoid him or her.

CHAPTER 14

1. This quote is taken from what is believed to be the sculptor's artistic testament, http://homepage.mac.com/emmapeel/rodin/rodin.HTML.

2. Sigmund Freud, "The 'Uncanny,'" in *Standard Edition,* trans. James Strachey (London: Hogarth, 1955), 17:217.

APPENDIX

1. Full quotation: "These things do I within, in that vast court of my memory. For there are present with me, heaven, earth, sea, and whatever I could think on therein, besides what I have forgotten. There also meet I with myself, and recall myself, and when, where, and what I have done, and under what feelings. There be all which I remember, either on my own experience, or other's credit." Augustine, *Confessions,* bk. 10, chap. 8. http://books.google.com/books?id=zDgLAAAAIAAJ&pg=PA174&lpg=PA174&dq=%22all+which+i+remember+either+on+my+own+experience%22&source=web&ots=sUf-zrch3X&sig=LGjPLOgj3eI2_sbSjJNSMNrajs0.

2. This is a game of three cards in which the dealer shows the player a target card, for example, the ace of spades, along with the jack of spades and jack of clubs. The dealer then rearranges the cards quickly and asks the player to select the target card.

Bibliography

Adler, Alfred, *Le Sens de la vie* (Paris: Payot, 1950).

_____, *What Life Could Mean to You*, trans. Colin Brett (Oxford: One World, 1992).

_____, *Le journal de Claire Macht: Technique de la psychologie individuelle comparée* (Paris: Belfond, 1981).

Allende, Isabel, *Portrait in Sepia* (New York: HarperCollins, 2001).

Ancelin-Schützenberger, Anne, *The Ancestor Syndrome: Transgenerational Psychotherapy and the Hidden Links in the Family Tree*, trans. Anne Trager (London: Routledge, 1998).

Antier, Edwige, *Vive l'éducation! Ce qui doit changer pour que nos enfants retrouvent le goût d'apprendre* (Paris: Robert Laffont/Réponses, 2003).

ATD Quart monde, *Rapport moral 2004* (Paris:Quart monde, 2005).

Augustine, Saint, *Confessions* (Oxford: Oxford University Press, 1991).

Bergson, Henri, *Mind-Energy* (Basingstoke: Palgrave Macmillan, 2007).

Binswanger, Ludwig, *Introduction à l'analyse existentielle* (Paris: Minuit, 1971).

Cardinal, Marie, *Les Mots pour le dire* (Paris: Le Livre de poche, 2004).

Céline, Louis-Ferdinand, *Journey to the End of the Night* (New York: W.W. Norton & Company, 1983).

Changeux, Jean-Pierre, *Neuronal Man: The Biology of Mind* (New York: Pantheon, 1985).

Cyrulnik, Boris, *Un merveilleux malheur* (Paris: Odile Jacob, 1996).

Damiani, Carole, "La Prise en charge des personnes traumatisées," *Culture en mouvement. Le débat*, n°35, March 2001.

De Lamartine, Alphonse, "Milly ou la terre natale,"*Les Harmonies poétiques et religieuses*, (Paris: Gallimard/La Pléiade, 1963).

De Saint-Exupéry, Antoine, *The Little Prince*, trans. Katherine Woods (New York: Harcourt, Brace & World, 1943).

Dilthey, Wilhelm, *Introduction to the Human Sciences*, trans. Ramon J. Betanzos (Detroit: Wayne State University Press, 1988).

Dumas, Didier, *Et l'enfant créa le père* (Paris: Hachette littérature, 2000).

Estrade, Patrick, *Comment je me suis débarrassé de moi-même: Les sept portes du changement*, (Paris: Robert Laffont: 2004).

_____, *Comment je me suis débarrassé de moi-même. Les sept portes du changemen*, (Paris: Robert Laffont/Réponses, 2004).

_____, "Pédophilie: les murs du silence," *Féminin Psycho*, special issue, spécial Parents, 2004.

_____, *Un reflet d'infini* (Paris: Dervy, 2000).

Forward, Susan, *Toxic Parents: Overcoming Their Hurtful Legacy and Reclaiming Your Life* (New York: Bantam Books, 1989).

Freud, Sigmund, *Essais de psychanalyse* (Paris: Payot, 1975).

_____, *The Interpretation of Dreams*, trans. A.A. Brill (New York: Macmillan, 1913).

_____, *La Technique psychanalytique* (Paris: PUF, 1953).

_____, *On Dreams, The Standard Edition* (New York: W.W. Norton & Company, 1965).

_____, *The Uncanny, Standard Edition,* trans. James Strachey (London: Hogarth Press, 1955).

_____, *Psychopathology of Everyday Life* (New York: Norton, 1965).

García Márquez, Gabriel, *Living to Tell the Tale* (New York: Knopf, 2003)

Guedeney, Antoine, *Ces enfants qui tiennent le coup. Donner du sens à une expérience insensée* (Revigny-sur-Ornain: Hommes et Perspectives, 1998).

Guenard, Tim, *Tagueurs d'espérance* (Paris: Presses de la Renaissance, 2002)

Hamilton, Hugo, *The Speckled People* (London: Fourth Estate, 2003).

Hesse, Hermann, *Siddhartha, Demian and Other Writings* (New York: Continuum, 1999)

Jung, Carl Gustav, *L'Âme et la Vie* (Paris: Buchet/Chastel, 1963).

_____, "The Personal and Collective Unconscious," in *The Collected Works of C.G. Jung,* ed. H. Read, M. Fordham, G. Adler, and Wm. McGuire, Bollingen Series 20 (Princeton: Princeton University Press, 1953–1979).

_____, *Psychologie de l'inconscient* (Geneva: Librairie de l'Université, Georg & Cie, 1978).

Kafka, Franz, *The Complete Stories* (New York: Schocken, 1971).

Ketchum, Katherine, and Loftus, Elizabeth, *The Myth of Repressed Memory* (New York: St. Martin's Press, 1994).

Kundera, Milan, *The Art of the Novel* (New York: Grove Press, 1986).

_____, *Identity* (New York: HarperCollins, 1999).

Lopez, Gérard, "L'Enfant dans son environnement," *Progrès en pédiatrie,* No. 17, Pédiatrie sociale (Rueil-Malmaison: Doin Éditeurs, 2004),

Luft, Lya, *Losses and Gains* (London: Vermilion, 2007).

Maslow, Abraham, *Toward A Psychology of Being* (Princeton, N.J.: Van Nostrand, 1968).

Merleau-Ponty, Maurice, *Phenomenology of Perception* (New York: Routledge, 2002).

Miermont, Jacques, *Dictionnaire des thérapies familiales. Théories et pratiques* (Paris: Payot, 1987).

Miller, Alice, *The Truth Will Set You Free: Overcoming Emotional Blindness and Finding Your True Adult Self* (New York: Basic Books, 2001).

Mitscherlich, Alexander, *Society Without the Father: A Contribution to Social Psychology* (New York: Harper, 1992; original work published 1963).

Molière, *The Bourgeois Gentleman* (New York: Applause Theatre Book Publishers, 1987).

Nasio, J.D., "L'Œdipe: un mythe indispensable," *Journal des Psychologues,* September 1994.

Nietzsche, Friedrich, *Beyond Good and Evil* (Amherst, N.Y.: Prometheus Books, 1989).

———, *Daybreak: Thoughts on the Prejudices of Morality*, ed. Maudemarie Clark and Brian Leitner (Cambridge: Cambridge University Press, 1982).

Nuber, Ursula, "Die sieben Sünden des Gedächtnisses," *Psychologie Heute* (Weinheim: Julius Beltz Verlag, October 2004).

Olivier, Christiane, *Jocasta's Children: The Imprint of the Mother* (London: Routledge, 1989).

Rank, Hugo, *The Trauma of Birth* (New York: Harcourt, Brace, 1929).

Rattner, Josef, *Die Kunst, eine Lebensgeschichte zu lesen*, Miteinander lebenlernen, Zeitschrift für Tiefenpsychologie, Gruppendynamik und Gruppentherapie, n°5, September 1983.

Ricoeur, Paul, *Memory, History, Forgetting* (Chicago: University of Chicago Press, 2004).

Robert, François, *Les Termes philosophiques* (Paris: Marabout, 1990).

Rovee-Collier, Carolyn, and Adler, Scott, "La mémoire," La Recherche, 267 (suppl.).

Rufo, Marcel, *Œdipe toi-même* (Paris: Le Livre de poche, 2002).

Servan-Schreiber, David, *The Instinct to Heal* (Emmaus, Pa.: Rodale Books, 2004).

Simonnet, Dominique, *Vivent les bébés! Ce que savent les petits d'homme* (Paris: Le Seuil/Points actuels, 1983).

Tadié, Jean-Yves and Marc, *Le Sens de la mémoire* (Paris: Gallimard/Folio, 1999).

Villemus, Philippe, *J'ai oublié* (Paris: Desclée De Brouwer, 2004).

Von Hofmannsthal, Hugo, *Three Plays: Death and the Fool, Electra, The Tower*, trans. Alfred Schwartz (Detroit: Wayne State University Press, 1966).

Yourcenar, Marguerite, *Lettres à ses amis et quelques autres* (Paris: Gallimard/Folio, 1997).

Zweig, Stefan, *Freud* (Paris: Stock, Stock Plus, 1978).

Acknowledgments

Writing a book on the interpretation of childhood memories is an exciting experience because the subject interests everyone. Some topics irritate people and others make them uncomfortable. This one brings them together. It's a lively topic that encourages people to think and talk, even to each other. Each time I mentioned the project, I would see something light up in the eyes of the person I was talking to. Within moments, he would say, "When I was little. . . " "You won't believe it, but . . ." or "My first memory dates back to . . ." followed by a personal story. Memories are always stories of self—stories in and of themselves, in the primary meaning of the term. Whether funny, sad, fantastic, unbelievable, phenomenal or ordinary, we play the leading role because they involve our personal experience.

When you happen to pick up a book in the bookstore, you can't imagine how much energy, synergy and determination went into it unless you've written one yourself. Many people—some close to me and others more removed—supported, helped and encouraged me in my research and writing. They helped me clarify, refine, frame and reframe the concepts of the method presented here, particularly when my explanations were unclear. None of this would have been possible without them. They include all those people closest to me whose gift is to stand by me, appreciate and love me every day. They help me, care for me, keep me healthy and boost my morale. The next group includes all those involved, directly or indirectly, in developing a book and getting it out into the world—the publisher, editor, proofreader, sales reps, reviewers and bookstores. Finally it is you, the reader, who truly brings this book to life. I cannot think of all these people without profound emotion. Now that the book is finished and is about to be launched, I am so grateful to them.

This is my twelfth book and I loved writing it. Writing always involves upheaval and anguish, but the experience also transports and transforms me. I grow with each one. This project caused me some very unpleasant moments and some awful weekends. I don't regret a single one. My family, friends and acquaintances have been extremely caring and kind throughout and I want to thank them all.

I would also like to thank the following people who agreed to participate in this voyage into the world of childhood memories. First, the members of the organization L'école de la vie, for their friendship, loyalty and energy in leading the support groups I founded more than twenty years ago.

Mary, Valerie, Marie-Claire, Corinne, Danielle, Kathrin, Henry, Bertrand, Gerald, Gabriel, Dennis, David and Bernard, who allowed me to tell their stories.

241

Bruno Quelen, president of Éditions 360, for his continuing and warm encouragement and the excellent wine we enjoyed during our last conversations about my book and everything else.

Nathalie Le Breton, my editor at Éditions Robert Laffont, whose faith and encouragement managed to keep my anxieties in check and my moods steady. She worked with me to shape this book and helped it ripen.

Véronique Aubry, my press agent at Éditions Robert Laffont, who also served as coach, strategist and adviser.

Corinne Marotte, my liaison with Nathalie Le Breton.

Patric Nottret, author of the novel *Poison vert*, who during a discussion at the 2003 book fair in Roquebrune-Cap-Martin drew my attention to Gabriel García Márquez's memoir, *Living to Tell the Tale*. I developed the outline for this book after reading and thinking about Márquez's memoir.

Gilbert Lugara, Panorama du Livre's media manager, who helped me refine my method *in vivo*. He insisted that the chapters on wounds deserved a lot of space. I think he was right.

Dr. Marc Bouchoucha, homeopath and careful reader of my work, for his encouragement, friendship and trust for more than twenty years.

Pierre-Jean Ollier, for the memories he gave me on the way back from his triathlon training. He helped me think about resistance differently.

Josette Guillot, one of the first people to really engage with my manuscript. Her outspoken feedback was as useful to me as a session with my own therapist. I am also grateful for her warm hospitality in Corsica at an important moment in the writing of this book.

Jean-Paul Hamon, for his valuable comments during an unforgettable run one morning along the ocean in Nice, the exchange of views and the hands-on exercises.

Élisabeth Hamon, for her critical and sensitive reading of my manuscript as well as her corrections and comments. I never would have dared ask her to do all that work, which she undertook graciously.

Dr. Christian Lallot, for opening his archives and unearthing important scientific journals that were enormously helpful in checking certain theoretical passages.

Marc Ferrari, for welcoming me to his beautiful adopted home of Brazil in the summer of 2005, for translating articles and book extracts from the Portuguese and for his friendship.

Child psychiatrist Dr. Philippe Parnot, for his friendly but rigorous assistance with certain psychological and medical terms, his constant availability and his keen and instantly analytic judgment.

Dental surgeon Dr. Sylviane Debroise, the first subject who really tried my method for analyzing and interpreting childhood memories while seated at a table in a Chinese restaurant in Paris, some fifteen years ago.

Yves Estrade, Annick Béroul, Joëlle Attard, my brother and sisters, for the wonderfully contradictory memories and the perplexing and disconcerting versions of events and places from my early childhood. They enabled me to observe, in situ, the importance of subjective perception in dealing with memories.

My son, Arthur Estrade, for his willingness to test my method for analyzing and interpreting memories and his continuing concern about the "global" success of my book. He respected the time I needed to set aside to think, as well as my moments of irritation when the book was not moving ahead as I hoped.

My wife, Huguette Estrade, for her many readings and rereadings of draft chapters and her critiques, evaluations, reframing and fine-tuning. She got me back on track when my text threatened to lose the reader. I would also like to thank her for helping me maintain a connection with the outside world during these months spent hibernating. Half the credit for this book goes to her.

Paul Vitti, the hero of *Analyze This,* played by Robert De Niro, for inspiring the chapter on guilt.

And for the American edition, I would like to thank all the staff and extra collaborators of Da Capo Lifelong for their precious work. In particular Chrisona Schmidt, copyeditor; Cisca L. Schreefel, Senior Project Editor; and Courtney Napoles, Assistant Editor.

Gregory Messina and Benita Ezard from the Foreign Rights Department at Robert Laffont in Paris for their marvelous work and contribution to the success of this book all over the world.

Leah Brumer for the superb translation of my book that she has realized and for her kind collaboration.

Matthew Lore, my editor in the United States, for his enthusiasm and total confidence in my book.

Resources

L'École de la Vie

I founded this nonprofit organization in 1997. Its mission is to increase public knowledge about psychology and culture. It organizes support and discussion groups that meet regularly. L'École de la Vie, Maison des Associations, Place Garibaldi, 06000 Nice.

Talks and Seminars

I have organized talks and seminars in conjunction with the publication of this book. Some are open to the public and others are intended for psychologists and those in the helping professions. More information is available on my website, www.patrickestrade.com.

www.souvenirs-souvenirs.blogspot.com

This blog is intended as an anonymous setting for those who would like to share their memories, whether painful, sad, moving or funny. It is a place to record memories, not a forum for dialogue. If you would like to record a personal memory there, you may email me at pg.estrade@free.fr or send me a postcard. I will be happy to post all memories that respect privacy and observe the rules of common courtesy.

About the Author

Psychologist and psychotherapist Patrick Estrade trained at the Analytic Psychology Institute in Berlin. The author of more than a dozen books, he holds seminars and conducts training sessions throughout Europe. Estrade lives in Nice, France, where he has a private practice.

Index